Christopher Maule

A Future for Economics

More Encompassing, More Institutional, More Practical

John Chant	Don McFetridge
Ehsan Choudhri	Christopher Maule
Steven Langdon	Gilles Paquet
Harvey Lithwick	Georg Rich

| Collaborative Decentred Metagovernance Series

This series of books is designed to define cumulatively the contours of collaborative decentred metagovernance. At this time, there is still no canonical version of this paradigm: it is *en émergence*. This series intends to be one of many 'construction sites' to experiment with various dimensions of an effective and practical version of this new approach.

Metagovernance is the art of combining different forms or styles of governance, experimented with in the private, public and social sectors, to ensure effective coordination when power, resources and information are widely distributed, and the governing is, of necessity, decentred and collaborative.

The series invites conceptual and practical contributions focused on different issue domains, policy fields, *causes célèbres*, functional processes, etc. to the extent that they are value adding to sharpening the new apparatus associated with collaborative decentred metagovernance.

This thirteenth volume in the series focuses on economics – a discipline fundamentally concerned with effective coordination, but one that has evolved significantly over the last half century. It presents the reflections of eight senior members of the economics profession who have all taught at some time at Carleton University in Ottawa, and therefore share a certain Carleton spirit characterized by a high degree of critical thinking and a deep commitment to making economics socially and politically useful. The Carleton Eight have operated from quite different quarters in the broad field of what used to be called political economy, and have experienced differently the pulls and pushes of their discipline over the last 50 years. Indeed, most of them have transformed their practice accordingly. We have asked them to speculate on the evolution of economics from their own perspectives, and on how it might contribute to ensuring more effective coordination and better governance in the future.

Interested parties are invited to join the Chautauqua.

Other titles published by INVENIRE are listed at the end of this book.

– Editorial Board
Caroline Andrew
Ruth Hubbard
Daniel Lane
Gilles Paquet (Chair)

Part 1.

Broad Trends

About Hedgehogs and Foxes
By Gilles Paquet

"The fox knows many things, but the
hedgehog knows one big thing."
Archilochus

Introduction

I n the 1950s, Isaiah Berlin published a short book, entitled
The Hedgehog and the Fox (a title inspired by the Greek
poet, Archilochus), where he categorized thinkers into two
categories: those whose emblem might be the fox with all his
cunning, and those whose emblem might be the hedgehog with
its unbeatable weapon: when threatened, rolling itself up into a
ball with sharp spines outward.

Reflecting on the evolution of economics over the last while,
Jean Tirole (winner of the Nobel Prize in Economics for 2014),
in his book, *Économie du bien commun* (2016), suggests almost as
a throw-away remark *en passant* that while in the distant past
(pre-World War II) economists were more fox-like, some 40 years
ago most of them had turned into hedgehogs, fully engrossed
by their competitive model. Then, Tirole reflects, the growing
complexity of the environment and a growing awareness of the
limitations of their big idea appear to have led economists to
drift back to a world of foxes (*Ibid.*: 142-146). Tirole is somewhat

equivocal as to whether this is an entirely desirable move. *À contrario*, I am quite unequivocal: this last drift is a welcome return to sanity, for any big idea, however big, is a handicap when it becomes an *idée fixe*.

A silent revolution

When I joined Carleton's Economics Department in the early 1960s, the discipline was in the midst of a silent revolution in Canada. On the one hand, we had the glorious tradition of "Canadian Economics" – applied economics in action in a world of foxes dedicated to the design of an economics that would fit the frontier country Canada was. This had dominated the scene since the 19th century, and had had its heyday in the second quarter of the 20th century. On the other hand, this was slowly being replaced by what might be labelled "economics in Canada" (a label invented by Harry Johnson), connoting the professional use of economics as a discipline by a contingent of hedgehogs who happened to be located in Canada (Neill and Paquet 1993).

Responding to the pressures of the Baby Boom, Canadian universities were massively hiring, and one could begin to see the balance in economics departments in North America shifting in favour of the hedgehogs. By the 1970s, it was the angle of vision (the economic perspective) that was the dominant feature of the tribe, rather than the appreciation of concrete "economies as instituted processes", à la Karl Polanyi (1957).

Carleton, being nestled in the nation's capital, and its economics department having a founding quartet of full-time faculty members (Tom Brewis, Ted English, Scott Gordon and Steve Kaliski) who were deeply involved in policy issues, took a prudent and balanced approach to the new wave. But even Carleton began to hire hedgehogs.

It is not that that the old core team and the first wave of newcomers in the 1960s were not well groomed in 'scientific economics'. This was never in question. But the prevailing cosmology of the group was somewhat foxy: it regarded economics as a powerful instrument, designed to improve the

Christopher Maule

A Future for Economics

More Encompassing, More Institutional, More Practical

John Chant	**Don McFetridge**
Ehsan Choudhri	**Christopher Maule**
Steven Langdon	**Gilles Paquet**
Harvey Lithwick	**Georg Rich**

INVENIRE

Ottawa, Canada
2017

INVENIRE © 2017

Library and Archives Canada Cataloguing in Publication

A future for economics : more encompassing, more institutional, more practical / edited by Christopher J. Maule; John Chant, Don McFetridge, Ehsan Choudhri, Christopher Maule, Steven Langdon, Gilles Paquet, Harvey Lithwick, Georg Rich.

Issued in print and electronic formats.
ISBN 978-1-927465-36-3 (softcover).--ISBN 978-1-927465-37-0 (HTML)

1. Economics. I. Maule, Christopher J., 1934-, editor

HB171.F88 2017   330   C2017-901643-1
                                                 C2017-901644-X

Invenire would like to gratefully acknowledge the ongoing support for this series by the Centre on Governance, University of Ottawa.

Published by Invenire
P.O. Box 87001
Ottawa, Canada K2P 1X0
www.invenire.ca

Copyediting by McE Galbreath
Cover design by Sandy Lynch
Layout and design by Sandy Lynch
Printed in Canada by Imprimerie Gauvin

Distributed by:
Commoners' Publishing
631 Tubman Cr.
Ottawa, Canada K1V 8L6
Tel.: 613-523-2444
Fax: 888-613-0329
sales@commonerspublishing.com
www.commonerspublishing.com

Table of Contents

Introduction 1
Christopher Maule

PART I   **Broad Trends**

About Hedgehogs and Foxes 5
Gilles Paquet

An Experience Characteristic of the Times . . . 17
Harvey Lithwick

Deepening of Development Economics 25
Steven Langdon

PART II   **Trade, Productivity and Institutions**

Evolution of Trade Theory 39
Ehsan U. Choudhri

Innovation and Productivity Growth 47
Don McFetridge

Multinational Enterprises 59
Christopher Maule

PART III   **Money and Finance**

Out of the Ivory Tower 71
Georg Rich

Financial Institutions in Canada 79
John Chant

About The Authors 91

About the Centre on Governance 95
  of the University of Ottawa

Introduction

Steve Ferris is responsible for initiating a series of monthly luncheons at Flippers Restaurant for retired members of Carleton University's Economics Department. While the conversation frequently involved common aging issues, economic topics were often raised as well. On reflection, it seemed that there was a certain accumulated wisdom that might be tapped and might even be useful to future generations considering the investigation of the study of economics. A common concern in our discussions has been the way economics has evolved, thus, the title of this dossier, *A Future for Economics*.

Retired members of the department were contacted, and eight agreed to draft a short piece which would reflect on this theme, based on their field of interest and experience over the past almost 60 years. No attempt is made to summarize these statements, but a word might be useful to put this exercise in context, and to explain why the department has been a congenial setting for teaching and research, and a milieu that has encouraged critical reflection on the evolution of the discipline.

Scott Gordon was appointed as the first member of Carleton's Economics Department in 1948. His breadth of scholarship influenced subsequent appointments, first Tom Brewis, Ted English and Steve Kaliski in the 1950s. A festschrift for Scott Gordon outlines these early years. Gilles Paquet joined in 1963 and became chairman from 1969 to

1972, during which time many of the current contributors were appointed – five went on to serve as chair. Gilles was later Dean of Graduate Studies and Research, maintaining his interest in and influence on appointments.

Different branches of economics were well represented in the department, as well as different approaches, leading to a wide variety of findings and policy recommendations. These results were discussed and commented on in a collegial way, and this led to wide-ranging debates. The department was not a place for doctrinal conflict, but one where ideas were robustly debated, sharpened and fine-tuned for publication.

Department members were active in providing advice to royal commissions, government committees and departments, as well as acting as consultants to public and private sector organizations. Undoubtedly members benefitted from these activities, but so did the students taught and supervised by those who had contact with the real world. The focus was always on what happened and why.

The authors have addressed *A Future for Economics* in a variety of ways, combining their academic and other professional experiences with developments that have taken place in the discipline, to suggest what the future directions might be. Examples provided range from advice given to the Swiss National Bank and to Bedouin tribes in the Middle East.

On a personal note, I would like to thank my colleagues for their contribution and Gilles Paquet for his support and for making it possible to publish these papers in www.optimumonline.ca and in book form. The whole process from contacting authors originally to publication took less than eight months.

Christopher Maule

understanding of what was going on in order to improve the human condition. The 'discipline' was never allowed to become an instrument of chastisement. Everyone was more or less Deweyan: "in the beginning was the issue."[1]

Carleton's Economics Department carried a robust whiff of critical thinking, and there was constant provocation by the external environment in Ottawa that kept us also in daily contact with the economic policy machine (royal commissions, Senate and House of Commons committees, etc.). This prevented the department from falling prey to the new reductive but seductive gospel of formalized, mathematized and quantophrenic economics.

By the end of the 1970s, hedgehogs had won the war against the foxes in economics departments in most of North America. By that time, a number of economists were beginning to feel sufficiently uncomfortable with the new gospel that had begun to migrate to the various interdisciplinary schools or institutes that had sprung up like mushrooms in most universities. It was that move that kept old style economics alive at the university. Indeed, the "college of economists" at Carleton grew substantially in size, but it was no longer located in only one place. It was diffracted in a flurry of units and locales where practical work, management, administration, and policy issues remained the focal points. At Carleton, this diffractive movement prevented an unduly abrupt dis-incarnation of the economics in practice. Economics in the old grand manner was sideswiped by an economics that was akin to engineering, but it did not disappear.

Enclaves as survival strategies

The silent revolution was both tonic and toxic: tonic, in the sense that it drove the fake out of some segments of the work of the

---

[1] The power of critical thinking of the old arsenal had been proven by the impact of Scott Gordon's pamphlet (Gordon 1961), exposing misdeeds of the Governor of the Bank of Canada. It led to the dismissal of the Governor. Gordon was the intellectual leader of the Department at Carleton in those days and his heretical spirit was a powerful driving force.

foxes; but also toxic, as it drove to quasi-extinction some sub-branches of economics that depended on important work in organizational and institutional economics. More dramatically, the silent revolution desiccated economics: it dried it out and deprived it of its human moisture. So a whole portion of the college of economists that could not find a way (or did not care to find a way) to graft itself onto the real human economy became absorbed in interesting puzzle-solving games that had little to do with concrete economies.

This desiccation period was celebrated by those in the discipline who suffered from physics envy. The new economics was regarded as a coming of age of economics as a true science – couched in theorems and lemmas. Elegance became a new metric replacing the older ones – relevance and usefulness. But this period was bemoaned by those who saw the economics journal becoming devoid of much relevance for practical affairs and policy. Economic history, comparative economics, law and economics programs, economic development, management schools, etc. became refuges for economists not fitting the new mold.

In those fringe locales at the margin of the central arenas, one did not feel too brutally the brunt of those critical years: pragmatic and eclectic approaches continued to be in good currency in laboratories where 'real economies' remained of central import, and where organizational and institutional design continued to be the focal point of interest. It was also in these locales that exploration and innovation in practical economics were most strongly encouraged. The key concern there was how our socio-economies (micro, meso, macro) should be redesigned to make them more heuristically effective. This was a world in which foxes thrived.

This important work out of the mainstream fed on inputs from the budding area of organizational science (Herbert Simon), from psychology (Daniel Kahneman), but also from the renewal of economic history (Douglass North), and from work on information and the design of governance mechanisms (Oliver Williamson, Elinor Ostrom, Thomas Schelling, George

Akerlof) – these were all foxes, all future Nobel Prize winners in economics who, however, had for quite a long time to live more or less on the margins of centre-stage, standard economics.

Indeed, at the time, one could be trained in economics at excellent graduate schools without ever hearing many of these names, and others, for those mentioned above are only meant to be a sample. Much creativity bubbled in the underground for years, while overground the official economics establishment was experiencing an epiphany of scientificity but also, at the same time, a crisis of confidence. For the hedgehog economists as professionals were slowly losing their dominance in policy fields to other professionals who were more fox-like.

Desiccated hedgehog economics as an unduly constraining corset

The new wave of hedgehog economists invaded economics departments, and this new orthodoxy infiltrated hiring and promotion committees, and, with a short lag, it created a demand for more hedgehogs. 'Old economics' was somewhat delegitimized, and a new fundamentalism emerged, giving to the word "discipline" – when applied to economics – a connotation that was very close to the one it had had in medieval times, when it referred to a whip or other instrument of self-inflicted chastisement used by certain orders of monks for mortification.

Economic models – the new formal reality – had taken a Quixotic turn. Like Don Quixote, too many economists had come to assume that "the idea that represents the world is truer than the world represented by this idea" [my translation] (Onfray 2014: 10-11).

Early on, this reductive view of the world was mocked from within the profession (Leijonhufvud 1973). By the 1980s, the discipline was denounced as slowly crippling the practice of economists (Katousian 1980). Wassily Leontief (a Nobel laureate in Economics) was even nastier. In a letter to the editor of *Science* on July 9, 1982, he chastised (1) his colleagues for having abandoned economics as an empirical science dealing with phenomena of common experience, and (2) departments of economics for imposing the new orthodoxy with means that "occasionally remind one of those employed by the Marines to maintain discipline on Parris Island" (Leontief 1982; Paquet 2009: 24).

All the Cassandras carrying the message of the costs of the impending decline of mainstream economics could not break down the robust cognitive dissonance of the hard-wired disciplinarian hedgehogs in control.

And yet, a serious appraisal of the economics profession in the empirical world of the 1970s and 1980s would reveal how grossly inadequate the profession's performance had become. In particular, it would document gross macro-policy failures that constituted a true *descente aux enfers* that took a full decade to recover.

Counter-revolution: the foxes are back *en force*

Fortunately, the market works – slowly and imperfectly at times – but it works. The hedgehog economics led not only to a greater and greater disconnectedness between economics and its practitioners, but also to a growing disenchantment for graduate studies in the new style economics which did not appear to hold much glorious promise of exciting employment. This, in turn, led to a loosening of the grip of hedgehogs on leading departments of economics, leading journals and leading funding councils.

This process was slow and is still very slow. Indeed many citadels (and not necessarily the most prestigious ones) are still controlled by hedgehogs – but fox economists have begun to find ways to work themselves back into positions of authority, to create new fora and new platforms, and to begin to rebalance the hedgehog-fox equation in the various colleges of economists. That is the good news. The bad news is that the fundamentalism virus that has so disserved economics departments is now observed to have contaminated certain cognate sectors.

What is undeniable is that the last 25 years have witnessed something of a renaissance of foxes in a plurality of economics departments – emerging from those enclaves where they had survived the onslaught of the 25 years before, or from the margins where they had thrived under different banners, or from refurbished departments of economics that had considerably broadened their cosmologies.

This renaissance cannot be understood without:

- a recognition of the resilience of the fox-like tradition that has survived *malgré tout* in the university world, and has continued to actively contribute to the corpus of work in economics;
- the persistence of foxes in mud time (as Robert Frost would call it), relentlessly exposing the "cracks in the walls of the citadel the hedgehogs were building";
- an acknowledgement of the important contribution of fox-like economists to the refurbishment of the discipline, either by borrowing eclectically from other disciplinary toolboxes, or by engaging in joint work with experts of other disciplines. Such works led to "a systematic transformation of the usual assumptions of standard economics models"; and
- an appreciation that this refurbishment generated "new sub-branches" of economics that have emerged or re-emerged from this generalized cross-fertilization – such as the new institutional economics and behavioural economics.

In all this work, fox economists have maintained a Deweyan attitude (in the beginning is the issue), and have partnered with lawyers, psychologists, organizational scientists, and the like, or have operated from their locales.

New institutional economics

The old institutional economics is associated with the names of Thorstein Veblen, John R. Commons and Karl Polanyi in North America in the late 19th and early 20th centuries

(Chavance 2009). It had lost much space to the neo-classical tradition in the first half of the 20th century, but remained a force to contend with in certain fields like economic history, and in certain regions like the southern part of the United States.

While it lost more ground during the silent revolution, this was probably one of the families of economics that profited most from the desiccation of economics: it was most effective in drawing attention to the flaws of a disincarnated economics, and it generated an effervescence of reactions to the silent revolution that coalesced around the new label "new institutional economics" – a field ranging all over evolutionary institutionalism, governance, and contractual arrangements, particularly dynamized by the works of Coase, Williamson and Schelling, among others, as illustrated in Ménard and Shirley (2005) or in more recent explorations in governance studies (Paquet 2013; Paquet and Wilson 2016).

Behavioural economics

This branch emerged from the interaction with psychology in the early days when *homo economicus* was exposed as a very flawed ideal-type, as a "rational fool" (Sen 1977). But Sen's paper *per se* had little impact on the profession. It took time before the seed planted by Harvey Leibenstein (Franz 2007), George Akerlof (1970), and many others had transformed into a full-fledged field called behavioural economics (Altman 2006; Cartwright 2011; Kahneman 2011; Thaler 2015).

All this revealed how much hedgehog economics had been constraining, how much economics could learn from foxes.

Some of this work has already received accolades from Nobel, but most importantly, these families of practitioners have contributed by their imagination and creativity to shaking off the *rigor mortis* of hedgehog economics, and have dynamized the sort of exploration and 'trespassing' that Albert Hirschman (1981) was calling for.

These are only illustrations of the fruits of the revival of fox-like economics. It is not possible to be exhaustive in a few pages. I leave it to my colleagues in specialized fields and areas in economics to identify the most significant contributions of the recent past by inspired economists – work that would need to be celebrated because it will be of significance for the sort of economics likely to be alive and well in the future. Their specialized expertise will allow them to better modulate the relative importance of hedgehogs and foxes in the sort of economics that is in the process of emerging in those subfields.

Quo vadis?

There was little optimism about overcoming the limitations of hedgehog economics in the complaints of Katousian and Leontief, or in the mocking of Leijonhufvud some 30 or 40 years ago. This is no longer the case. Yet the return of the foxes has not generated exuberance, and students in economics are not widely invited to boldly tackle new cross-disciplinary problems.

Economics departments continue to suffer from a high degree of conservatorship and hysteresis. The personnel of hedgehogs who has been hegemonic has left its imprint on the profession. The battle line is now at the hiring process in economics departments, and, in the trenches, where there is still some resistance when graduate students in economics insist on pursuing their research in unorthodox, fox-based alleys.

So, interested budding economists may still have, for a while, to indulge in sophisticated searches to find a place of quality that encourages foxes to operate freely and creatively at the frontiers of economics. Such places exist where research programs based on economics, organizational and behavioural sciences are opening new trails – in cross-disciplinary schools but also in economics departments like the one developing new approaches to epistemic rationality as a way to cope with complex and uncertain worlds (Grandori 2013). But very many good economics departments remain ill-equipped and uninterested in supporting research programs in those emerging fields.

Gilles Paquet is an economic historian and a specialist in institutional economics and governance. He has also done extensive work in the media. He taught in the Department of Economics at Carleton from 1963 to 1981. He later joined what is now the Telfer School of Management at the University of Ottawa, where he created the Centre on Governance in 1997. He has been the President of the Royal Society of Canada, and he is a Member of the Order of Canada. His website is found at www.gillespaquet.org.

References

Akerlof, George. 1970. "The Market for 'Lemons': Quality, Uncertainty, and the Market Mechanism," *Quarterly Journal of Economics*, 84: 488-500.

Altman, Morris (ed.). 2006. *Handbook of Contemporary Behavioral Economics*. Armonk, NY: M.E. Sharpe.

Berlin, Isaiah. 1957. *The Hedgehog and the Fox*. New York, NY: Mentor.

Cartwright, Edward. 2011. *Behavioral Economics*. New York, NY: Routledge.

Chavance, Bernard. 2009. *Institutional Economics*. New York, NY: Routledge.

Frantz, Roger. 2007. *Renaissance in Behavioral Economics – Essays in Honor of Harvey Leibenstein*. New York, NY: Routledge.

Gordon, H. Scott. 1961. *The Economists versus the Bank of Canada*. Toronto, ON: Ryerson Press.

Grandori, Anna. 2013. *Epistemic Economics and Organization – Forms of Rationality and Governance for a Wiser Economy*. New York, NY: Routledge.

Hirschman, Albert O. 1981. *Essays in Trespassing – Economics to Politics and Beyond*. Cambridge, UK: Cambridge University Press.

Katousian, Homa. 1980. *Ideology and Method in Economics*. New York, NY: New York University Press.

Kahneman, Daniel. 2011. *Thinking Fast and Slow*. New York, NY: Farrar & Giroux.

Leijonhufvud, Axel. 1973. "Life among the Econs," *Western Economic Journal,* 11(3): 327-337.

Leontief, Wassily. 1982. "Academic Economics," *Science*, vol. 217, July 9, p. 104-107.

Ménard, Claude, and Mary M. Shirley (eds.). 2005. *Handbook of New Institutional Economics*. New York, NY: Springer.

Neill, Robin F. and Gilles Paquet. 1993. "L'économie hérétique: Canadian Economics Before 1967," *Canadian Journal of Economics*, 26(1): 3-13.

Onfray, Michel. 2014. *Le réel n'a pas eu lieu – Le principe de Don Quichotte*. Paris, FR: Autrement.

Paquet, Gilles. 2009. *Crippling Epistemologies and Governance Failures: A Plea for Experimentalism*. Ottawa, ON: The University of Ottawa Press.

Paquet, Gilles. 2013. *Tackling Wicked Policy Problems: Equality, Diversity and Sustainability*. Ottawa, ON: Invenire.

Paquet, Gilles and Christopher Wilson. 2016. *Intelligent Governance: A Prototype for Social Coordination*. Ottawa, ON: Invenire.

Polanyi, Karl. 1957. "The Economy as Instituted Process" in K. Polanyi *et al.* (eds.). *Trade and Markets in the Early Empires: Economics in History and Theory*. New York, NY: Free Press, p. 243-270.

Sen, Amartya. 1977. "Rational Fools: A critique of the behavioral foundations of economic theory," *Philosophy and Public Affairs,* 6(4): 317-344.

Thaler, Richard H. 2015. *Misbehaving – The Making of Behavioral Economics*. New York, NY: Norton.

Tirole, Jean. 2016. *Économie du bien commun*. Paris, FR: Presses Universitaires de France.

An Experience Characteristic of the Times

By Harvey Lithwick

In the beginning

I began my graduate studies at a particularly exciting time and place. In 1960, the Kennedy presidency had begun, and its impact on Harvard University's Department of Economics was profound. Many of the faculty's bright stars not only played key roles in the election campaign, but immediately after the installation of the new president, began work on a wide range of policy papers.

Since regular classes were given by these professors, they regularly commuted between Cambridge and Washington, and their enthusiasm about their policy work was infectious. The single most important venues at Harvard were their open seminars, in which policy ideas were put forth for discussion and analysis with their colleagues and students alike.

What struck me at the time was the wide range of issues that these economists were being called on to help the new administration address, many of which lay outside our conventional emphasis on aspects of the domestic and international economy, and in particular, economic growth and stability, and international trade and finance. Those new, broader concerns included poverty and race, health, education, the environment, defense, and law and order.

Although I began my graduate study with an interest in Third World economic development, I found the field conceptually and practically limited with one exception, and that was the emerging interest in the historical empirical record and the statistically calculated determinants of economic growth in advanced societies. As a result, I chose to write my Ph.D. dissertation under the superb guidance of Simon Kuznets on the subject of economic growth in Canada.

Based on that work (which was published soon after by the University of Toronto Press), and immediately upon graduation, I was recruited to the staff of The Royal Commission on Taxation, which held out the possibility of a strong, if traditional, public policy focus. The research staff consisted mostly of traditional economists, and the high level of interest in tax reform at the time led me to believe that we might be able to come up with major policy initiatives that could help accelerate Canada's economic growth.

Coming to Carleton and the Ottawa nexus

Quite by chance, shortly after I arrived in Ottawa in 1973 to work on the Royal Commission, I dropped in on the Carleton University, Department of Economics, and I met with Scott Gordon, Tom Brewis, Ted English and Steve Kaliski. I was somewhat familiar with their work, which most of all focused on high profile public policy issues, such as Gordon's recent, very public attack on the role of the Governor of the Bank of Canada. They suggested I teach a class for them in my spare time, although, at the time, I had evinced little interest in a teaching career.

To my complete surprise, I loved the teaching and the fact that a group of similar minded young, mostly policy-oriented faculty was being recruited simultaneously – T.K. Rymes, Gilles Paquet and Irwin Gillespie. When I was offered a position, I quickly accepted. By the end of my first full-time year, we were a department, most of whose members were not only actively engaged in public policy research and teaching, but also acutely aware of the need to play a role in wider fora to help energize public debates on many of these broader, newly emerging issues.

I believe that, at the time, such an emphasis was unique in economics departments and it was particularly appealing to me. And the flexibility of the Department allowed me to complete my Royal Commission work at the same time.

In those early years, 1964-69, I collaborated closely with all three other members of the new team. I wrote a paper with Tom Rymes and George Post of the Bank of Canada on economic growth – a rare collaboration between academic economists and top officials at the time. Irwin Gillespie prepared a monograph for me as part of the Urban Canada study (see below). But my closest and most fruitful collaboration was with the Gilles Paquet force of nature.

One of the 'downsides' of our small size and this emphasis on policy was a shortage of staff members who were trained in and willing to teach statistics. Paquet convinced me to join him in developing a course which combined theory and practice by means of case studies and homework assignments that sharpened my own skills in the subject, and proved (surprisingly) to be popular with students. Best of all, I had found someone who was as obsessed with public policy as I was, and was even more 'catholic' than I in the areas in which he was interested.

Meanwhile, new public policy issues were shaping the post-Kennedy landscape in the US and had a spillover effect on us. Primary among these issues were the urban crisis and the massive destruction of swathes of American cities. Paquet and I collaborated to study the emerging literature in urban economics, and then to publish what I believe was the first study in that field in Canada with the title "Urban Studies: A Canadian Perspective". In it, we argued for a multi-disciplinary approach to this new (for economists) policy area – an approach that remains anathema to many classically trained economists. As a direct consequence of that publication, I was asked by the Government of Canada to head up a task force to propose policies to help it not only to better understand urban dynamics in the country, but to provide practical guidelines that might help it steer a constructive course for dealing with the consequences of those changes.

To do so, and to the chagrin of my family, I had to interrupt my just beginning sabbatical leave in Israel and return to Ottawa for a seven-month period, during which time the problem was defined, a solid team of scholars working independently was recruited, and the work was completed. The final volume, *Urban Canada: Problems and Prospects*, was published by the Government of Canada, accompanied by five monographs ranging in subject matter from housing, transportation, the urban public economy (by Irwin Gillespie), urban poverty, urban transportation, and a final forward-looking monograph on strategies for the urban future.

Nor did this body of work get filed away in the archives. I had the opportunity to present it in person to then Prime Minister Trudeau, in a challenging and rewarding interchange, and then to his Cabinet a bit later. Apparently the recommendations struck a receptive chord, for within a few months, a new independent Ministry of State for Urban Affairs, was created with a full time Minister, Robert Andras. Mr. Andras asked me to help him set up the new ministry, and Carleton took the unusual step of giving me permission to take another year's leave of absence to do so.

Unfortunately, in the middle of this exciting development, the Quebec separatist crisis erupted. Some of our proposals called for a federal role as facilitator of important programs and policies in collaboration with the provinces, but due to the Quebec situation, politics dictated that such an innovation, with its complex constitutional implications, had to be taken off the table. When it became clear to me that the subject itself would now necessarily be given much lower priority by the government, both in terms of the status of the ministry and the limited resources allocated to it, I decided to return to Carleton and pursue my academic work, while exploring other challenging fields of public policy.

So while I cannot claim my urban policy work had any long run, public policy impact in institutional terms, the fact that these issues were now being publicly debated, based on more substantial economic analysis, was very gratifying, and I will forever be grateful to Carleton, and, in particular, my colleagues in the Department of Economics for providing an environment that allowed me this opportunity to combine my research work and public policy activity.

Next steps

Other collaborative opportunities emerged at about the same time, i.e., the mid to late 1970s. The newly created Economic Council designated Canadian economic growth as a major field of interest, and I was able to work with them. Simultaneously, the Science Council was focusing on science policy with an emphasis on technological change. I consulted with them in several areas of overlapping interest, and in particular, the sources of productivity growth; out of that association came my study on science policy and the economy.

After being burned with the federal urban initiative due to the Quebec crisis, the federal government began to focus on a broader mandate *vis à vis* the provinces, which it subsumed under the newly created Department of Regional Economic Expansion. This time, one of the mistakes of the past was corrected, and a high level Minister, Jean Marchand, was appointed to lead the generously financed department.

I had already been shifting my own research focus in that direction, partly influenced by the earlier work of Tom Brewis. To survey the emerging field of regional policy, I edited a book of newly published papers with the title *Regional Economic Policy: The Canadian Experience*. Shortly thereafter, there began a series of collaborations with the new department, and I succeeded in publishing a variety of papers on federalism and regional policy, and regional policy analysis.

The silent revolution

Since my arrival, the Department of Economics at Carleton had undergone dramatic changes. Initially offering strictly an undergraduate program, our rapid growth enabled us to launch an MA program by the early 1970s, driven mainly by the ambitions and interests of the "gang of four". Thereafter we began a prolonged effort to add a Ph.D. program with a public policy emphasis. Because our sister university, the University of Ottawa was attempting to develop a Ph.D. program in economics of its own, we were "encouraged" by the province of Ontario to cooperate with it in the name of efficiency and to develop a joint Ph.D. program.

Needless to say, this was a labourious effort given the radically different cultures of the two departments, but eventually the program got off the ground. By that time, our own department had become a large one, with all traditional fields covered by very promising scholars. But a subtle change had taken place – a relative de-emphasis of policy broadly defined, and a felt need to emulate the typical structure of economics departments found in the larger and better known universities.

Greater emphasis was placed on advanced statistics and econometrics, mathematical economics, and economic theory. All these were, of course, necessary for a competitive graduate program, but the free-wheeling diversity of the Department's earlier incarnation was being constrained. Ph.D. students who wanted to work on policy issues were finding it difficult to find the courses they would have preferred and, more important yet, to get thesis advisers who shared their interest.

My personal response in 1981 was to take a joint appointment with Carleton's School of Public Administration, which itself was beginning to take off in terms of size, and had the added attraction of having on staff a good number of policy-oriented economists, many of whom had joint appointments or at least teaching commitments with the Department of Economics.

In the new environment, I was able to continue close collaboration with my colleagues at the School and with some very bright graduate students. Together, we published a number of reports and articles in a surprisingly wide range of subjects. We built a new program in Development Administration, with students from third world countries, that continues to this day. One result was making new contacts with colleagues in international development agencies such as the World Bank, the UN Development Program, the OECD and CIDA, and again a range of papers followed. This new orientation eventually led me into my final field of policy analysis, namely policy evaluation, with a heavy emphasis on cost-benefit analysis, which has continued to this day.

The evolution of the field

I have dwelled on my policy interests because I sense that this broader, almost political-economy orientation is largely out of fashion in contemporary economics departments.

I believe my own experience suggests that the reason is not because there has been no demand for this type of research, but because the discipline of economics has become more insulated from the world of public policy, broadly defined. This is a discipline-wide phenomenon and is not restricted to Carleton University as my more recent experience indicates.

By 1990, my wife and I decided to move permanently to Israel, where we had previously spent several wonderful sabbaticals. Yet even in Israel, where once economists played key roles in the political economy of the nation, the field was becoming more technical, more inward-looking, and highly motivated to be competitive with the best departments abroad.

I was fortunate to be asked to work with a colleague to create a new entity, The Negev Center for Regional Development, at Ben-Gurion University of the Negev, where it was possible to extend my interests in regional development policy to a new range of issues, from water scarcity to environmental degradation. The final area of research in this milieu was a study of the local, urban Bedouin population and its socio-economic developmental prospects.

Conclusion

In retrospect, I was fortunate to be able to work and conduct research at a very special department at Carleton University at a very unique time. Times have changed and universities, including Carleton, have evolved. Moreover, with the growth and professionalization of government, there is much less perceived need for outside collaboration, a development that I think is unfortunate.

One advantage being on the outside has conferred on me, and I suspect on many others, was the ability to study and appreciate policy challenges that face those on the inside. I had to negotiate with provincial and municipal political and institutional leaders who taught me much about the real world issues they faced and the many unanticipated (by me) difficulties they had to deal with in proposing and implementing often elegant, but unrealistic, policy ideas put forward by well-intentioned academics. But working with these people also allowed me and my colleagues to see things somewhat more objectively and, therefore less defensively, allowing us to provide honest criticism, something that has been lost in the increasingly bureaucratized, risk-avoiding world of the public service. Such an advantage may be viewed as a threat from those inside, but only by the egotistical and the insecure.

Harvey Lithwick began his teaching career at Carleton University in 1963, and served as Chairman of Carleton's Economics Department (1974-77). He was recruited by the Canadian government in 1969 to undertake a study of urban Canada and was appointed Assistant Secretary to create the Ministry of State for Urban Affairs. He was a Visiting Professor at the Hebrew University in Jerusalem in 1969-70 and 1977-78. In 1992, he moved to Ben-Gurion University of the Negev in Israel where, with Professor Yehuda Gradus, he helped set up the Negev Center for Regional Development until his retirement in 2005.

Deepening of Development Economics

By Steven Langdon

D evelopment economics emerged in the period after World War II, with a predominant focus on analyzing and reducing the large gap in living standards between richer and poorer countries in the world. As such, economic development was understood as requiring the acceleration of economic growth rates in poorer countries so that they could "catch up" with richer nations. Structural change was usually seen as crucial for this to take place (such as industrialization to shift labour out of what was seen as low-productivity agriculture). The challenges in raising growth rates became the preoccupation of most research – how to increase capital accumulation, using trade to expand output per capita, maintaining macro-economic balance, inducing industrial investment. In recent years, however, this emphasis on economic growth has shifted dramatically, and development economics has transformed itself as an area of study.

Why this change in focus? Because growth does not get rid of poverty

The main reason for this change of focus is the recognition that widespread poverty remains prevalent in many countries where average GDP per capita has gone up significantly, and rates of growth have increased. Such resource exporting countries as Nigeria and Zambia, for instance, have relatively high average per capita incomes now, yet still show well over 60 percent of their populations living in poverty in 2010-13 (according to World Bank definitions based on deprivation relative to "basic human needs" per household). The poverty lines that the Bank measures across countries use purchasing power parity calculations of household per capita consumption of US$1.25 per day as their norm.[1] For 35 African countries as a group (during an extended period of considerable growth in the continent), such poverty calculations show 21 nations with over 40 percent of their people below such severely constrained levels.

Nobel Prize winning development economist A.K. Sen has broadened the notion of poverty further. "Poverty is not just a lack of money," he says. "It is not having the capability to realize one's full potential as a human being."[2] Applying this 'capabilities approach', the United Nations has developed a human development index (HDI) to provide a different perspective on development than GDP per capita measures. It has deepened this with a multi-dimensional poverty index (MPI), reflecting 10 indicators (including household consumption per capita, but also extending to malnourishment measures, maternal and child mortality rates, school attendance and years of education). By this measure of 35 African countries with data, 25 have 50 percent or more of their populations living in poverty. The African total reaches 477 million; along with 632 million in India and 159 million in Bangladesh and Pakistan, over 1.2 billion people show major evidence of national deprivation.[3]

Poverty is important in new frameworks of development economics not just because of the hardship it represents; a focus on it as a primary concern can also lead to different

---

[1] Ravallion (2010) provides a detailed discussion of World Bank poverty lines and the ways in which they are measured. In the most recent measurements, the World Bank's poverty reference level has increased to US$1.90 daily per capita.

[2] For more detailed commentary by him, see Sen 2016.

[3] The details of MPI calculation and country results are found at www. hdr.undp.org.

policy analysis directions than an emphasis on growth. Recent research in six African countries, for instance, has shown that agricultural gains reduce poverty headcounts by more than similar-sized industrial production gains; and food crop growth benefits the poor much more than export crop gains – a five percent improvement in food crop output in Ethiopia, for instance, has a greater poverty reduction result than an 18 percent improvement in export-crop production (Diao *et al.* 2010). Such findings contradict past conventional wisdom that industrialization should be a priority, and that export crops are an optimal path toward development.

Other researchers have examined such factors as inflows of foreign direct investment (FDI) from a poverty perspective, also reaching different conclusions than usual suggestions that increasing FDI contributes to higher national economic growth. Econometric analysis of changing foreign investment and HDI data for 52 African countries over 1990-2007 finds that there are regions (Southern Africa and Francophone West Africa) where more FDI seems to worsen HDI levels (Gohou and Soumaré 2012). FDI in resource and import-substitution sectors in these areas appears to be widening inequalities, skewing benefits to small minorities, and leaving most people worse off in terms of human development indicators.

Gender inequality at the heart of poverty

Development economics has also found that gender inequality is often at the heart of persistent poverty. Women are widely prevented from improving resource usage on land they farm by limits on their control of that land; inheritance laws sometimes prevent property going to widows; poor local infrastructure forces women into excessive time allocations to obtain water and firewood; women are under-represented in decision-making institutions; maternal mortality rates are very high; and access to education is lower for women than for men (UN Women 2015). In responding to serious poverty concerns, the World Bank, the International Monetary Fund and the governments of developing nations in 1999 initiated country Poverty Reduction Strategy Papers (PRSPs), agreed between the international financial institutions (IFIs) and individual national governments, providing financing for detailed policy efforts against poverty; within these, reducing gender disparities has come to be emphasized as a crucial priority.

The focus on gender inequality has also led to new statistical means of tracking development indicators to reflect gender concerns. The OECD (Organisation for Economic Co-operation and Development), for instance, has developed a social institutions and gender index that examines women's access to land and to bank loans, women's freedom of movement, violence against women and inheritance rights. With 1 showing complete inequality and 0 indicating complete gender equality, the average 2009 measure for South Asia is .300, North Africa is at .272, Sub-Saharan Africa at .183 and South America at just .014 (IFAD 2011). The UN has also developed several indicators, built on the statistics used to calculate the HDI and MPI, but focused on women. The gender-related development index (GDI) compares country HDI levels for women against those for men, deriving the average result for women as a percentage of the result for men across the three sets of indicators within the HDI. (The highest result for Africa, for instance, is in Botswana where women's HDI result is .964 of that for men – significantly better than in Mali with its GDI of .771).

Another measure, the gender inequality index (GII), is based on women's reproductive role (maternal mortality rates and adolescent birth levels), women's empowerment (levels of parliamentary representation and secondary school enrollment), and women's labour force participation. For the GII, the lower the index, the greater the equality between women and men. A number of European countries (Slovenia at .016, Switzerland at .028 and Germany at .041) have particularly low GIIs, based on low adolescent birth rates, low maternal mortality and virtual gender equality in higher education – much better results than the average of .739 for South Asia and .735 for Sub-Saharan

Africa. Of 29 countries with 2013 data available in Africa, only Mauritius (at .375) is below the .400 level.[4]

A gender focus, particularly as part of a poverty focus, also leads to differences in policy analysis. The difficulties women have in accessing traditional sources of capital compared to men have led to significant new micro-credit initiatives aimed at women – based as well on evidence that women perform especially well in repaying such small loans. The Grameen Bank in Bangladesh successfully launched such efforts with rural women, and their example has since been pursued in dozens of poorer countries. Another initiative with significant gender dimensions in most countries has been the quickly spreading use of social cash transfers (SCTs) to directly benefit poor target households in rural areas where food insecurity deprivations are high. First used in a major way in Brazil, SCTs have proliferated across Africa since 2005, operating in 37 countries there by 2013. On average, the programs transfer some 20 percent of existing base consumption levels to severely disadvantaged rural households, with an overall bias toward poorer, women-headed households and pregnant mothers. Not all SCTs are focused in that direction (some aim at orphans from families of HIV-AIDS victims), but most show poor rural women as the main recipients.[5]

Governance – another source of poverty

A third new focus for development economics has been the question of governance – what factors make for effective, responsive and efficient governmental systems able to implement improved policies to overcome poverty and gender inequality? The World Bank has been a leader in exploring

[4] The details of GDI and GII calculation and country results are at www. hdr.undp.org.

[5] Ethiopia's Productive Safety Net Programme, with 8 million recipients, is the largest African SCT initiative, with Tanzania's Productive Social Safety Net system reaching 5 million people. Research on the effects of SCTs in Ghana, Malawi, Tanzania and Ethiopia show particular gains for vulnerable rural women. For more details, see Thome *et al.* 2016.

this broader, political-economy context in a rigorous and quantitative way, analyzing various statistical indicators that are associated with better rule-of-law records. The Bank has also stressed anti-corruption measures, working with countries to establish autonomous agencies able to oversee government activities such as Auditors-General, Parliamentary Public Accounts Committees and integrity bureaus (like Botswana's Directorate on Corruption and Economic Crime).

Other researchers have worked on establishing a theoretical understanding of the state structures and functions that seem to have had such success in parts of Asia (and elsewhere) in both accelerating industrialization and economic growth rates and, at the same time, very considerably reducing poverty levels. The concept of "developmental states" has been identified – "essentially mobilizing states in which political and bureaucratic components have been virtually fused" (Leftwich 1995). Autonomous from many domestic interests and nationalistic in dealing with external forces, these states have used assertive policies on education, land reforms, trade subsidies and public investment to build industrial economies and reduce poverty.

Zambian economist Charity Musamba (2010) has outlined four features of developmental states: 1) they have a "development-oriented political leadership" with the "sustained political will to govern the market in accordance with development aspirations;" 2) they are characterized by autonomous and effective bureaucracies able to forge business alliances and implement efficient interventions, reflecting merit-based appointment systems and institutional safeguards against corruption; 3) they maintain support from people because of their records of rapidly expanding economies and because they stress "high levels of commitment to poverty reduction;" 4) they are usually characterized by "a production-oriented private sector," prepared to expand investment and improve technology in close collaboration with bureaucrats. Such states in Asia have usually been marked by weak civil society pressures, safe-guarding their policy autonomy (examples are

South Korea, Singapore and Taiwan). But Musamba suggests that successful developmental states in Africa must be more democratic in character, so as to enforce accountability from governance institutions. Strong civil society intervention, for instance, has reinforced government action against HIV-AIDS in Botswana, improved health care in Uganda through the use of Citizen Report Cards and worked to upgrade educational quality in Tanzania and Kenya.[6]

Environmental threats at the core of development

More recently, there has been a fourth new focus in development economics – the environmental threats that are increasing for poorer countries in the context of global climate change. Environmental concerns were not a focus in earlier economic development research but became more significant as increasing air and water pollution combined with land degradation in poorer countries; a "greening" of the World Bank took place as well as the launch of the United Nations Environmental Programme (UNEP) with its headquarters in Africa (Nairobi, Kenya). New work measuring environmental externalities in social cost-benefit analysis and analyzing the dynamics of common property resources reflects this shifting emphasis.[7]

The momentum of global climate change, driven in large part by man-made greenhouse gas (GHG) emissions (especially of carbon), deepens the significance of environmental pressures. The scientific Intergovernmental Panel on Climate Change

[6] *Uwezo* (Swahili for "capability") is a civil society initiative in East Africa that has carried out a series of rounds of educational testing, beginning in 2009, to evaluate the quality of learning in primary schools (Uwezo 2013). Citizen Report Cards were used in 2005 to successfully encourage improvement in primary health care facilities in parts of rural Uganda – such initiatives have since spread widely to other countries (Björkman and Svensson 2007). For information on the role of civil society groups in Botswana's effective response to HIV-AIDS, see Avert 2016.

[7] See, for instance, Hardisty's (2010) application of social cost-benefit analysis to a selection of environmental pollution protection options in North Africa. For an example of research on common property resources, examining the case of the Lake Kafue fisheries in Zambia, see Haller and Chabwela 2009.

(2014) shows global warming has been taking place (with an increase of some 0.8° Celsius since the pre-industrial period), and this has been associated with wider rainfall variation and more extreme weather events. It also projects with high confidence that these trends will accelerate in the years ahead and that human populations face large risks of serious damage. Water shortages, flooding and pollution are likely to worsen, as are crop yields in drier regions, disease burdens (particularly from the spread of malaria), and malnutrition. Women and children are the most vulnerable to these risks, especially in rural areas of poorer countries.

Africa contributes a very small share of GHG emissions (five percent of that from high income countries), but it is at particularly high risk from climate change, facing rising temperatures of 2 to 4° Celsius by 2100, with consequent heat, drought and flooding consequences. Effective adaptation strategies are very costly to achieve, unless global-level agreements can reduce the rate of global warming – so Africa has had to become vigorous in advocating world carbon policy changes, as well as becoming more active in countering emission levels through set-asides of forest reserves.

Conclusion

Overall, these major shifts in focus make development economics a dynamic new terrain. The field has taken on a changing set of dimensions for research and analysis; some like the environment linking to the work of natural scientists, others like governance connecting to law and political science. New theoretical perspectives are being explored that reflect this, with vibrant debates over such questions as the potential dynamism of small-scale agriculture, how to measure environmental externalities as public goods and what can be done at the community level to spur gender equality and improve human development.[8]

---

[8] See, for example: Harris and Orr (2014) on whether small-scale farming can have wide enough effects on improving the incomes of poor households to reduce country poverty levels significantly; Graves (2007) on the difficulties

After World War II, new intellectual challenges led to the emergence of development economics. Now those challenges have been deepened, promising an exciting and substantive future for the field.

Steven Langdon was a member of Carleton's Economics Department from 1974 to 1984. He also taught at the Norman Paterson School of International Affairs. Then he accepted a position as Associate Director for Economics and Rural Development at the International Development Research Centre (IDRC); this followed two years on leave as IDRC Regional Program Officer for Social Sciences in Eastern and Southern Africa, based in Nairobi. His further research and project implementation has focused on poverty reduction, industrial restructuring and governance. After serving as an MP for nine years, he worked with the World Bank and the Parliamentary Centre in 20 different African countries as well as a number of countries in Asia and Latin America. He is now an Adjunct Professor in the Economics Department at Carleton and is completing a textbook on African economic development for a UK publisher.

References

Avert. 2016. *HIV and AIDS in Botswana*. London, UK: www.avert.org.

Björkman, M. and J. Svensson. 2007. "Power to the People: Evidence from a Randomized Field Experiment of a Community-Based Monitoring Project in Uganda," Policy Research Working Paper 4268. Washington, DC: World Bank.

Diao, X., P. Hazell and J. Thurlow. 2010. "The Role of Agriculture in African Development," *World Development*, 38(10): 1375-83.

that social cost-benefit analysis has in measuring environmental externalities and the questions this raises about the value of the methodology; Gandhari and Mutsau (2014) on whether women's savings clubs at the local level can spur wider gender equality in the Gokwe area of Zimbabwe.

Gandhari, E. and S. Mutsau. 2014. "The Dynamics of the Gendered Division of Labour in Agro-Forestry: A Case Study of Njelele Ward III in Gokwe Zimbabwe." In Asuelime *et al.* (eds.). *Selected Themes in African Development Studies.* Geneva, CH: Springer International Publishing, p. 59-76.

Gohou, G. and I. Soumaré. 2012. "Does Foreign Direct Investment Reduce Poverty in Africa and Are There Regional Differences?" *World Development,* 40(1): 75-95.

Graves, P.E. 2007. *Environmental Economics: A Critique of Benefit-Cost Analysis.* Lanham, MD: Rowman and Littlefield Publishers.

Haller, T. and H.N. Chabwela. 2009. "Managing common pool resources in the Kafue Flats, Zambia: from common property to open access and privatization," *Development Southern Africa,* 26(4): 555-567.

Hardisty, P.E. 2010. *Environmental and Economic Sustainability.* Boca Raton, FL: CRC Press.

Harris, D. and A. Orr. 2014. "Is rainfed agriculture really a pathway from poverty?" *Agriculture Systems,* 123, p. 84-96.

IFAD (International Fund for Agricultural Development). 2011. *Rural Poverty Report 2011.* Rome, IT: IFAD.

Intergovernmental Panel on Climate Change (IPCC). 2014. *Climate Change 2014 Synthesis Report.* Geneva, CH: IPCC.

Leftwich, A. 1995. "Bringing Politics Back In: Towards a Model of the Developmental State," *Journal of Development Studies,* 31(3): 400-427.

Musamba, C. 2010. "The Developmental State Concept and its Relevance for Africa." In P. Meyns and C. Musamba (eds.). *The Developmental State in Africa - Problems and Prospects.* Duisburg-Essen, DE: Institute for Development and Peace (INEF), Report 101/2010, p. 11-41.

Ravallion, M. 2010. "The Debate on Globalization, Poverty and Inequality: Why Measurement Matters." In S. Anand, P. Segal and J.E. Stiglitz (eds.). *Debates on the Measurement of Global Poverty.* Oxford, UK: Oxford University Press.

Sen, A.K. 2016. *Development Research and Changing Priorities.* United Nations University-World Institute for Development Economics Research (UNU-WIDER) Annual Lecture 19, Helsinki, www.wider.unu.edu.

Thome, K., J.E. Taylor, M. Filipski, B. Davis and S. Handa. 2016. *The local economy impacts of social cash transfers – A comparative analysis of seven sub-Saharan countries.* Rome, IT: FAO (Food and Agriculture Organization).

UN (United Nations) Women. 2015. *The Beijing Declaration and Platform for Action turns 20. Summary Report.* New York, NY: United Nations, p. 11, www.unwomen.org.

Uwezo. 2013. *Are Our Children Learning? Literacy and Numeracy Across East Africa.* Uwezo East Africa at Twaweza, Nairobi, www.uwezo.net.

PART II.

Trade, Productivity and Institutions

| Evolution of Trade Theory
By Ehsan U. Choudhri

In the beginning

n the mid 1960s, I attended the meetings of the American Economic Association in Chicago to participate in the job market for economists. My job interview with Steve Kaliski, then chair of Carleton University's Economics Department, was scheduled in the last slot at the end of the day. When I met him, we were both tired and instead of going through the typical interview routine, we ended up having a relaxed chat. I did not know then that I would receive an offer from Carleton University which I would accept and my professional career at Carleton would last over five decades.

Being an international trade specialist, I will first discuss key developments in international trade theory during my long tenure at Carleton, and then examine some basic policy issues, and conclude by expressing some thoughts about future directions of this field.

Key developments

When I started my career, the Heckscher-Ohlin model dominated the theory of international trade.[1] A key insight of this model is that an important source of international trade is international differences in relative factor endowments. A

---

[1] This model is based on the work of Swedish economists, Eli Heckscher and Bertil Ohlin.

simple version of the model with two factors, capital and labour, predicts that a capital abundant country (a country with a larger amount of capital per worker) would import labour intensive products (whose production requires less capital per worker). This prediction is intuitively appealing but seemed to be inconsistent with the evidence that in clearly capital abundant United States, industries competing with imports were, in fact, capital intensive.[2] Even the predictions of the more general Hecksher-Ohlin model, with multiple factors, were difficult to reconcile with empirical evidence, and it was generally recognized that the model needed to be extended to allow for international differences in productivity (Leamer 1980; Brecher and Choudhri 1982; Trefler 1995).

The Hecksher-Ohlin model was also challenged by two other facts. First, much of the global trade took place (especially before the recent rise of China as a major trading country) not between capital-abundant developed and labour-abundant developing countries, but among developed countries with similar incomes per capita and stocks of capital per worker. Second, contrary to the expectation of inter-industry trade (for example, export concentrated in capital-intensive and imports in labour-intensive industries), there was evidence of much intra-industry trade (substantial exports and imports in the same industry). Attempts to explain these facts lead to models that revolutionized international trade theory. An important feature of the new trade models is to assume that households consume differentiated goods produced under monopolistic competition (for example, Krugman 1980). This feature can explain intra-industry trade since there is a demand for varieties of imported goods both at home and abroad. Moreover, countries need not be different to have an inducement to trade with each other.

Appeal of the new trade models was enhanced by another development: the empirical success of the Gravity model of international trade. The traditional version of the Gravity

---

[2] This inconsistency was called the "Leontief paradox," and was based on the work of Wassily W. Leontief in 1953.

model showed that bilateral trade flows across trading pairs can be explained well by three variables: the GDPs of importing and exporting countries and the distance between the pair (a proxy for bilateral transportation costs). Modern versions of the Gravity model relate bilateral trade flows to a set of variables specific to either importing or exporting countries (instead of just GDPs) and to multiple indexes of bilateral trade costs. Although the Gravity model was not initially motivated by an international trade model, new trade models provide a solid theoretical foundation for the modern versions of the Gravity model (Anderson and van Wincoop 2003).

Studies based on firm data showed that only a portion of firms in an industry export their products, and the exporting firms tend to be more productive than non-exporting firms. A next generation of new trade models has emerged to explain these facts (Melitz 2003). Key features of these models are (ex-post) heterogeneous productivity across firms and fixed costs required for exporting. Given that firms incur additional costs to establish export operations, less productive firms in an industry may not find it worthwhile to export. Profitability of exports by a firm can differ across countries, and it is possible that no firms in an industry have an incentive to export to certain countries. This implication can explain why zero bilateral trade is observed for a large number of trading pairs (Helpman *et al.* 2008).

Policy issues

Recently, there has been much concern about the consequences of globalization. Globalization is broadly defined as the freer flow of trade, labour and capital around the world. In this paper, I will focus on the narrower topic of the effects of trade liberalization. There has been considerable controversy about whether a new or existing trade agreement represents a good or a bad deal for a country? In the recent presidential elections in the US, for example, doubts have been expressed about the desirability of entering the Trans Pacific Partnership (TPP) or staying in the North American Free Trade Agreement (NAFTA).

An important proposition implied by all trade models is that compared to isolation (no trade), free trade provides the potential for a country to enhance its consumption (consume larger amounts or greater varieties of goods) and thus gain from trade. Similar gains from trade are also available from freer trade arising from a reduction in trade costs. Thus, trade agreements that reduce trade costs by reducing or removing tariff or non-tariff barriers are beneficial for each trading partner. Then why is trade liberalization so controversial?

One possible reason is that trade liberalization is often associated with globalization, and there is opposition to immigration and foreign investment. There are also concerns about trade liberalization based on two important qualifications to the proposition on gains from trade. First, the proposition establishes a potential for gains from freer trade, but does not imply that freer trade will make everyone better off. Indeed, as discussed below, there is a strong possibility that some households will be worse off under freer trade. There is a potential for an economy to compensate all losers from freer trade and still be left with some benefits. However, sufficient compensation is typically not provided, and thus free trade agreements face strong opposition from groups that are adversely affected. Second, realization of efficiency gains from trade requires reallocation of resources between or within industries, and such adjustment may not occur smoothly. Indeed, in the short run, there may be a loss of jobs in the less productive industries or firms, and it may take some time for the unemployed to find new jobs. The unemployment problem may be worsened for a country where imports increase more than exports in the short run. These adjustment problems could be addressed by appropriate compensation/retraining schemes and macroeconomic policies, but adequate policy measures are generally not undertaken.

In the traditional model, trade alters the distribution of income between labour and capital. A major proposition –

known as the Stolper-Samuelson theorem[3] – states that freer trade would shift production from labour-intensive to capital-intensive industries in the capital abundant (high income) country, thereby reducing wages by lowering the demand for labour (and increasing the return to capital by raising its demand). The opposite effects would occur in the labour abundant country. An important implication of the theorem is that trade liberalization would not be good for labour in high income countries. However, there was significant trade liberalization from 1960s to 1990s through multilateral or bilateral trade agreements, but rich countries did not experience a decline in the real wage rate. One explanation of why trade did not harm labour in rich countries is that there was also significant technological progress in this period which improved labour productivity. Another explanation suggested by new trade models is that liberalization of trade between rich countries increased intra-industry trade which (unlike inter-industry emphasized by the traditional model) did not require a shift to more capital intensive production and thus did not lower real wages.

The college wage premium has increased significantly in many developed countries, especially since the 1990s. There is controversy about what factors caused this change. One view is that recent improvements in technology are biased towards skilled (college educated) labour, which raises the demand for skilled relative to unskilled (non-college) labour and leads to a higher college wage premium. An opposing view is based on the Stolper-Samuelson theorem, reformulated in terms of a model that focuses on the relative endowments of skilled and unskilled labour rather than on capital and labour. In this view, rich countries are abundant in skilled labour, and freer trade has moved production to skill-intensive industries and thus lowered unskilled labour wages and raised skilled labour wages in these countries. The argument between these views is

[3] This theorem was derived by Wolfgang Stolper and Paul Samuelson in 1941.

not settled. However, there is one piece of evidence that favours skill-biased technology explanation over trade explanation. It is observed that, contrary to the reformulated Stolper-Samuelson theory, college wage premiums have also gone up in some developing (abundant in unskilled labour) countries. This fact would be consistent with a world-wide technical change that favours skilled labour.

An important development in 2001 was the entry of China into the World Trade Organization (WTO), which allowed a major emerging country to have freer trade with developed countries. China's WTO membership was followed by rapid growth in China's trade with developed countries. Competition with imports from China also lead to a significant decrease of the manufacturing sector in developed countries. Manufacturing had been declining steadily in these countries for some time, but trade expansion with China accelerated this decline. Job losses in manufacturing in this period were more severe in that unemployed workers found it more difficult to find new jobs. The unemployment situation was exacerbated by the recession caused by the 2007 financial crisis. This evidence has been used to blame free trade agreements for manufacturing job loss in the US and other high-income countries. However, freer trade cannot account for the long-term contraction of the manufacturing sector in rich countries. A key source of this trend appears to be technological change which is shifting the comparative advantage of developed countries to new skill-intensive, non-manufacturing industries. Restricting trade would delay but not stop this shift in countries abundant in skilled labour. The experience of trade liberalization with China does underscore the lack of effective policies to compensate and retrain displaced workers, especially workers without a college education, who lost jobs in manufacturing and found it hard to find jobs in new types of industries.

Future directions

It is difficult to predict what new theoretical insights or empirical facts will have a major influence on the future development of international trade theory. I expect that in view of the recent experience, trade models would pay more attention to the effect of freer trade on the level and duration of unemployment. Also, I think that the link between trade and productivity growth would be explored further. In the new trade models, reductions in trade costs increase average productivity in an industry by shifting production from less productive, non-exporting firms to more productive, exporting firms. Earlier literature had emphasized the role of trade in transmitting useful knowledge and thus helping less productive countries to catch up with more productive ones. This mechanism represents another channel for freer trade to increase productivity and I expect that future development of new trade models would incorporate this channel.

There has been a major change in the methodology for research in international trade since I was a graduate student. When I was completing my graduate studies, although mathematics was increasingly used in international trade theory, there was very little empirical research in this field. My thesis had an empirical component, but it was based on a small data set which I assembled by visiting the library and it required little computer work. International trade models have now become very complex and often require sophisticated mathematical tools. Another major change has been the use of empirical research based on large data sets. This has been facilitated by the easy access to online data and advances in computing power. I think that this trend will continue and skills to process and analyze big data sets would be very useful for students planning to specialize in international trade.

Ehsan U. Choudhri joined the Department of Economics at Carleton University in 1965. He retired from the full-time teaching position at Carleton University in 2012 and is currently a Distinguished Research Professor. He has undertaken research on a wide range of topics in international trade and macroeconomics. His has published in many journals including Canadian Journal of Economics,

Journal of International Economics, Journal of Monetary Economics, Journal of Political Economy *and* Quarterly Journal of Economics. *He has held visiting positions at a number of institutions including University of California at Los Angeles, Rutgers University, Georgetown University, Bank of Canada and International Monetary Fund. He has served as chair of the Department of Economics at Carleton University and associate editor for the* Journal of International Economics.

References

Anderson, James E. and Eric van Wincoop. 2003. "Gravity with Gravitas," *American Economic Review*, vol. 93, p. 170-92.

Brecher, Richard A. and Ehsan U. Choudhri. 1982. "The Leontief Paradox, Continued," *Journal of Political Economy*, 90(4): 820-823.

Helpman, E., M. Melitz and Y. Rubinstein. 2008. "Estimating trade flows: trading partners and trading volumes," *Quarterly Journal of Economics*, 123(2): 441-487.

Krugman, Paul. 1980. "Scale Economies, Product Differentiation, and the Pattern of Trade," *American Economic Review*, vol. 70, p. 950-959.

Leamer, Edward E. 1980. "The Leontief Paradox, Reconsidered," *Journal of Political Economy*, 88(3): 332-349.

Melitz, M.J. 2003. "The impact of trade on intra-industry reallocations and aggregate industry productivity," *Econometrica*, 71(6): 1695-1725.

Stolper, W. and Paul A. Samuelson. 1941. "Protection and Real Wages," *The Review of Economic Studies*, 9(1): 58-73.

Trefler, Daniel. 1995. "The Case of the Missing Trade and Other Mysteries," *American Economic Review*, 85(5): 1029-46.

Innovation and Productivity Growth
By Don McFetridge

Introduction

We are said to have entered a period of slower growth in per capita incomes globally (Nordhaus 2016). A variety of reasons have been advanced for this but one of the most carefully documented is a slowdown in the rate of productivity growth.[1] While opinion varies as to how long this slowdown will continue, it has raised concerns about maintaining, let alone raising, the living standards of an aging population.[2]

Canada has a longstanding productivity problem. Both our productivity and our rate of productivity growth have historically been lower than the United States and a number of other advanced economies. The causes of this have been much studied by economists in universities, research institutes

---

[1] On the possibility that the observed slowdown is the result of a measurement problem, see Byrne, Fernald and Reinsdorf (2016), "Does the United States have a productivity slowdown or a measurement problem?"

[2] For three different views on the duration of the productivity slowdown, see Gordon (2016), *The Rise and Fall of American Growth: The U.S. Standard of Living since the Civil War*; Brynjolfsson and McAfee (2014), "The Dawn of the Age of Artificial Intelligence"; McCloskey (undated), "The Great Enrichment Came and Comes from Ethics and Rhetoric".

as well as numerous government departments, councils, commissions and agencies.[3]

A variety of explanations for Canada's comparatively poor productivity performance have been suggested over the years. There is a general recognition that a major source of productivity growth is innovation. Indeed, innovation is simply doing things better or, more precisely, making better use of the resources available to us and is thus synonymous with multi-factor productivity growth.

Innovation is often associated with scientific R&D. While this has been a useful theoretical abstraction, it can also be misleading when it comes to public policy discussions. Innovation can take on a variety of forms, including improvements in the design or governance of either private or public sector organizations or in managerial or regulatory practices or rule-making as well as technological improvements. Innovation is cumulative, building on experience. Innovation is interactive with inspiration coming from employees, customers, suppliers and either near or distant competitors as well as from formal research efforts. Important innovations need not be technologically, let alone scientifically, sophisticated.[4] Indeed, technological innovation can precede the development of the underlying scientific understanding of the phenomenon concerned.

Canada's innovation gap has tended to be viewed rather narrowly in terms of the technological sophistication of the business sector. The gap is manifest in a variety of ways. Technological innovations, advanced manufacturing technologies, in particular, diffuse more slowly in Canada than in other countries. Canadian businesses are less R&D-intensive than similar businesses in other countries. R&D-intensive industries constitute a smaller portion of the Canadian economy

---

[3] Most notable is the work done at the Centre for the Study of Living Standards and the Institute for Competitiveness and Prosperity, as well as the work done at Statistics Canada by John Baldwin and his colleagues.

[4] I am indebted to John Chant for suggesting the shipping container as an example. See Levinson (2006), *The Box: How the Shipping Container Made the World Smaller and the World Economy Bigger.*

than in other advanced economies. Canadian inventors account for a disproportionately small share of international patenting activity. There are relatively few large Canadian-based, high-tech "anchor tenant" firms. The public perception of Canada as an innovative nation has not been helped in recent years by the bankruptcy of Nortel, the collapse of Blackberry, and the endless demands of Bombardier for government support.

Does economics have anything to say either about the factors conducive to innovation in general or about the reasons for the apparent lack of innovation in Canada and our resulting poor productivity performance? During the 40 or so years that I have been teaching economics, economists have made considerable progress in understanding the extent to which the innovative process is influenced by economic incentives, in general, and public policy, in particular, rather than occurring autonomously. Below I highlight some of the major findings.

The economics of innovation

The impetus for treating innovation as an economic decision by firms and entrepreneurs came from Joseph Schumpeter who argued that competition from new product and process innovations and the "gale of creative destruction" that can accompany it has a greater impact on economic well-being than price competition, and that innovation is unprofitable if imitation is costless and immediate as is the case in a perfectly competitive market (Schumpeter 1942). Subsequently, Kenneth Arrow pointed out that a monopolist's incentive to innovate is also attenuated to the extent that product or process innovation would cannibalize its existing monopoly profits (the Arrow replacement effect). That is, having zero economic profits pre-innovation, a firm in a competitive market would have more to gain from innovation than a monopolist (Arrow 1962). This assumes that the monopolist is not threatened by outsiders who could also introduce the innovation concerned, and that the competitive firm could monopolize this innovation if it were to introduce it. Thus, the incentive to innovate depends on both the ability to appropriate the resulting rents and the contestability of the markets concerned (Shapiro 2012).

Economists have devoted considerable effort to developing Schumpeterian oligopoly and monopolistic competition models in which firms compete on the basis of innovation as well as price. This competition may take the form of a winner-take-all competition *for* a market (disruptive innovation), or of incremental innovation *within* a market, or of both incremental innovation within a market and disruptive innovation from outsiders.

An example of competition for the market is a patent race in which the first to invent takes the market (Loury 1979). An implication of patent race models is that there could be too much as well as too little innovative effort if the profitability of being first exceeds the net benefit of advancing the date of innovation.

Competition among incumbents to introduce incremental innovations has been modelled in a variety of ways.[5] One well-known model sees more intense competition as stimulating innovation under some circumstances and deterring it under others. That is, innovation may be both a way of escaping intense "neck and neck" competition and a way for laggard firms to obtain a share of collusive industry profits. This can imply an inverted U-shaped relationship between the intensity of competition and innovation (Aghion *et al.* 2005).

Improvement innovations build on their predecessors. The incentive for one step in the process can come at the expense of the other steps (Scotchmer 1991). The cumulative nature of innovation makes it difficult to assess an industry's dynamism from a snapshot. A concentrated market may be the result of intense competition for the market, but it may also retard future innovation.

Theoretical models of competitive innovation have been accompanied and informed by a vast array of empirical studies

---

[5] See for example, Baumol (2002), *The Free Market Innovation Machine: Analyzing the Growth Miracle of Capitalism.*

of the relationship between firm and industry structure, respectively, and either innovative activity or productivity growth (Cohen 2010). Empirical studies of the relationship between the intensity of competition and productivity itself find that increases in the intensity of competition (for example, from trade liberalization) increase productivity (Syverson 2011).

The view that profit-oriented, innovative activity is limited by the inability of innovators to appropriate sufficient profits from it implies that there is a gap between social and private rates of return from innovation (a positive externality) which can, in theory, be remedied by public policy. There has been a considerable amount of empirical research on the extent and incidence of what has become known as the R&D externality or R&D spillovers (Hall, Mairesse and Mohnen 2009). This research has involved economists in many countries and has become increasingly sophisticated over time.

The empirical literature on the R&D externality (to which the late Jeffrey Bernstein made a significant contribution while he was at Carleton) reveals that the excess of the social over the private rate of return on R&D can be very large but varies considerably across industries. With the advent of panel databases, it has become possible to delineate more fully the mode and geographical reach of spillovers from R&D and other measures of technological innovation. Does what goes on in Palo Alto stay in Palo Alto? Some studies find that technological spillovers are international while more detailed analysis finds that spillovers decay with distance.[6] Localized spillovers are likely the result of the inter-firm mobility of skilled employees.

Public policy towards innovation

Policy-related research has adopted a variety of methodologies. One approach is analytical, focusing on the case for, and most effective form of incentives for business sector innovation as

---

[6] Lychagin, Pinske, Slade and Van Reenan (2016), "Spillovers in Space: Does Geography Matter?" Using a panel data set of 1,383 US headquartered firms over the 20-year period ending in 2000, the authors find that technology spillover effects are significant but that they decay with distance.

well as ancillary intellectual property and industrial policies. Another approach is historical and institutional, describing the innovative process and the various institutions that participate in it (Mowery and Rosenberg 1989).

Analysis of the most effective form and magnitude of direct government support for business R&D draws on empirical evidence from many countries on both the magnitude of business sector R&D spillover benefits, and the responsiveness of firms to government R&D support (Zunega-Vicente *et al.* 2014). The most rigorous Canadian analysis finds that the federal Scientific Research and Experimental Development (SR&ED) tax credit passes a benefit-cost test but, due to high administration and compliance costs, two other R&D support programs do not (Lester 2012). These conclusions depend heavily on the assumed excess burden of the taxation required to finance government R&D support as well as the spillover and responsiveness parameters. Some economists have argued that the assessment of government support of business innovation should go beyond benefit-cost analysis (Lipsey and Carlaw 1998).

With respect to intellectual property, among the issues economists have addressed are the optimal duration and breadth of the patent right. A long patent term rewards the inventor but restricts access to the invention by both users and follow-on inventors. A short patent term does the reverse. A broad patent rewards the pioneering inventor but discourages follow-on inventions. A narrow patent does the reverse. The challenge is to define both breadth and term to provide sufficient incentive for both pioneer and follow-on inventions (Gilbert and Shapiro 1990). In some cases, open (user-led) innovation regimes under which successive improvements are freely available have proven successful (Von Hippel 2005).

Historical and contemporary case studies go "inside the black box" and examine the institutions involved and the nature of the linkages among them (Baldwin and Hanel 2003). This has led to the description of what have been called "national systems of innovation" and "local innovative clusters." The concept of a self-sustaining innovative cluster with universities, government labs and larger innovation-intensive (anchor tenant) firms, incubating and spinning off new start-ups which grow (scale up) and ultimately contribute spinoffs themselves, has become a central feature of public policy discussions in Canada and elsewhere (Institute for Competitiveness and Prosperity 2016).

The link between university research and business sector innovation has received considerable attention, perhaps too much in the view of some commentators (Lunvall 2005). The discrepancy between the strength of Canadian academic (university) research and the weak performance of the Canadian business sector with respect to innovation is frequently noted (Council of Canadian Academies 2013). It has long been contended that the considerable presence of foreign-owned firms has inhibited business sector innovation in Canada (Britton and Gilmour 1978). More recent analysis concludes that foreign-owned firms are no less engaged in domestic collaboration, no less outward-looking and, in general, no less innovative than are similarly-placed Canadian-owned firms (Baldwin and Hanel 2000). Ownership is not the issue. The domestic market environment, especially its regulatory balkanization, might be a better place to look for answers.

Innovation can be organizational as well as technological; it can occur in the public sector as well as the business sector; and it can also have redistributive effects. Organizational innovation in the public sector can be politically contentious – witness the current debates about the provision of health care, policies to reduce carbon dioxide emissions, home mail delivery and Uber cabs.[7] Interest group politics may stymie innovation leading to a "sclerotic" (low productivity growth) economy.

Some economists have blamed the US productivity slowdown on an increasingly politicized regulatory process (Cochrane 2016). A variety of other public policies protect laggard incumbent firms at the expense of potentially more productive entrants (Baily and Montalbano 2016). Political

---

[7] On health care, see for example, Dodge, Golden and Macklem (2016), "Millenials can't pay for boomer health care without productivity gains".

hostility to congestion pricing of public transportation infrastructure reduces productivity and increases capacity costs (Glaeser 2016). The apparent popularity of the notion of "social license" suggests that our problem is not so much a lack of innovation as our inability to accept it.[8]

Conclusions

In an open society with property rights and the rule of law, human ingenuity will out. An open society recognizes that innovation in public sector governance can complement technological innovation and enable it to accommodate rather than oppose creative destruction. Canada will be as innovative as we allow it to be.

Donald McFetridge was a member of the Department of Economics at Carleton from 1974 until his retirement in 2013. He specialized in Industrial Organization and Competition Policy. His research efforts while at Carleton benefitted immensely from collaboration with colleagues Keith Acheson, John Chant, Ed Hughes, Douglas Smith and the late Stanley Wong and also with some excellent graduate students, including Atipol Bhanich Supapol, Lin Bian, Ron Corvari, Aming He, Ashish Lall, Derek Olmstead, Mohammed Raffiquzzama and Eftichios Sartzetakis. He also learned a great deal from discussions at various times with colleagues Stephen Ferris, Soo Bin Park, Tom Ross and, of course, the late John McManus.

---

[8] The chronology of the Gordie Howe Bridge is illustrative. See https://www.wdbridge.com/en/chronology#/step-25.

References

Aghion, Phillipe, Nick Bloom, Richard Blundell, Rachel Griffith and Peter Howitt. 2005. "Competition and Innovation: An inverted U Relationship," *The Quarterly Journal of Economics,* 120 (May): 701-728.

Arrow, Kenneth. 1962. "Economic Welfare and the Allocation of Resources to Invention" in Universities-National Bureau Committee for Economic Research and the Committee on Economic Growth of the Social Science Research Councils (ed.). *The Rate and Direction of Inventive Activity: Economic and Social Factors.* Princeton, NJ: Princeton University Press, p. 467-492.

Baily, Martin and Nicholas Montalbano. 2016. "Why Is U.S. Productivity Growth So Slow?" Hutchins Center Working Paper #22, September. https://www.brookings.edu/wp-content/uploads/2016/09/wp22_baily-montalbano_final4.pdf [retrieved November 10, 2016].

Baldwin, John and Petr Hanel. 2000. "Multinationals and the Canadian Innovation Process," no. 151. Ottawa, ON: Statistics Canada, Microeconomic Analysis Division, June.

Baldwin, John and Petr Hanel. 2003. *Innovation and Knowledge Creation in an Open Economy: Canadian Industry and International Implications.* Cambridge, UK: Cambridge University Press.

Baumol, W.J. 2002. *The Free Market Innovation Machine: Analyzing the Growth Miracle of Capitalism.* Princeton, NJ: Princeton University Press.

Britton, John and James Gilmour. 1978. *The Weakest Link: A Technological Perspective on Canadian Industrial Underdevelopment* (Background Study no.43). Ottawa, ON: Science Council of Canada, Supply and Services Canada.

Brynjolfsson, Erik and Andrew McAfee. 2014. "The Dawn of the Age of Artificial Intelligence," *The Atlantic,* February 14. http://www.theatlantic.com/business/archive/2014/02/the-dawn-of-the-age-of-artificial-intelligence/283730/ [retrieved November 1, 2016].

Byrne, David, John Fernald and Marshall Reinsdorf. 2016. "Does the United States have a productivity slowdown or a measurement problem?" Brookings Papers on Economic Activity Conference Draft, March 10-11. https://www.brookings.edu/wp-ontent/uploads/2016/03/ByrneEtAl_ProductivityMeasurement_ConferenceDraft.pdf [retrieved September 15, 2016].

Cohen, Wesley. 2010. "Fifty Years of Empirical Studies of Innovative Activity and Performance" in Bronwyn Hall and Nathan Rosenberg (eds.). *Handbook of the Economics of Innovation.* North Holland: Elsevier, p.129-213.

Cochrane, John H. 2016. "Growing Risks to the Budget and the Economy: Testimony before the House Committee on Budget," September 14, p. 3. http://faculty.chicagobooth.edu/john.cochrane/research/papers/Cochrane_testimony_Sept_14_2016.pdf [retrieved September 15, 2016].

Council of Canadian Academies. 2013. "Paradox Lost: Explaining Canada's Research Strength and Innovation Weakness," Ottawa, ON: Council of Canadian Academies. http://www.scienceadvice.ca/uploads/eng/assessments%20and%20publications%20and%20news%20releases/synthesis/paradoxlost_en.pdf [retrieved November 4, 2016].

Dodge, David, Brian Golden and Tiff Macklem. 2016. "Millenials can't pay for boomer health care without productivity gains," *The Globe and Mail,* August 25. http://www.theglobeandmail.com/report-on-business/rob-commentary/millennials-cant-pay-for-boomer-health-care-without-productivity-gains/article31536679/.

Gilbert, Richard and Carl Shapiro. 1990. "Optimal Patent Length and Breadth," *Rand Journal of Economics,* 21 (Spring): 106-112

Glaeser, Edward. 2016. "If You Build It ...," *City Journal,* Summer. http://www.city-journal.org/html/if-you-build-it-14606.html [retrieved November 4, 2016].

Gordon, Robert. 2016. *The Rise and Fall of American Growth: The U.S. Standard of Living since the Civil War.* Princeton, NJ: Princeton University Press.

Hall, Bronwyn, Jacques Mairesse and Pierre Mohnen. 2009. "Measuring the Returns to R&D," NBER Working Paper 15622, December.

Institute for Competitiveness and Prosperity. 2016. "Clusters in Ontario: Creating an Ecosystem for Prosperity," Working Paper No. 26, June. http://www.competeprosper.ca/uploads/WP26_clusters_rev.pdf [retrieved November 4, 2016].

Lester, John. 2012. "Benefit: Cost Analysis of R&D Support Programs," *Canadian Tax Journal,* 60(4): 793-836 and the references therein.

Levinson, Marc. 2006. *The Box: How the Shipping Container Made the World Smaller and the World Economy Bigger.* Princeton, NJ: Princeton University Press.

Lipsey, Richard and Kenneth Carlaw. 1998. "A Structuralist Assessment of Technology Policies: Taking Schumpeter Seriously on Policy," Industry Canada Working Paper No. 25. Ottawa, ON: Industry Canada.

Loury, Glenn. 1979. "Market Structure and Innovation," *Quarterly Journal of Economics,* 93 (August): 395-410.

Lunvall, Bengt-Ake. 2005. "National Innovation Systems – Analytical Concept and Development Tool," Paper presented at the DRUID conference, Copenhagen, June 27-29. http://www.druid.dk/conferences/Summer2005/Papers/Lundvall.pdf [retrieved, September 15, 2016].

Lychagin, Sergey, Joris Pinske, Margaret Slade and John Van Reenan. 2016. "Spillovers in Space: Does Geography Matter?" *Journal of Industrial Economics,* 64 (June): 295-335.

McCloskey, Deirdre. "The Great Enrichment Came and Comes from Ethics and Rhetoric" (undated). http://www.deirdremccloskey.org/docs/pdf/IndiaPaperMcCloskey.pdf [retrieved November 5, 2016].

Mowery, David and Nathan Rosenberg. 1989. *Technology and the Pursuit of Economic Growth*. Cambridge, UK: Cambridge University Press.

Nordhaus, William. 2016. "Why Growth Will Fall," *New York Review of Books*, August 18. http://www.nybooks.com/articles/2016/08/18/why-economic-growth-will-fall/ [retrieved September 16, 2016].

Schumpeter, Joseph. 1942. *Capitalism, Socialism and Democracy*. New York, NY: Harper.

Scotchmer, Susan. 1991. "Standing on the Shoulders of Giants: Cumulative Research and the Patent Law," *Journal of Economic Perspectives*, 5 (Winter): 29-41.

Shapiro, Carl. 2012. "Competition and Innovation: Did Arrow Hit the Bull's Eye?" in Josh Lerner and Scott Stern (eds.). *The Rate and Direction of Inventive Activity Revisited*. Chicago, IL: University of Chicago Press, p. 361-410.

Syverson, Chad. 2011. "What determines productivity?" *Journal of Economic Literature*, 49 (June): 351-357.

Von Hippel, Eric. 2005. *Democratizing Innovation*. Cambridge, MA: MIT Press.

Zunega-Vicente, J., C. Alonso Borrego, F. Forcadell and J. Galan. 2014. "Assessing the Effect of Public Subsidies on Firm R&D Investment: A Survey," *Journal of Economic Surveys*, 28(1): 36-67.

Multinational Enterprises
By Christopher Maule

"Alice laughed. 'There's no use trying,' she said.
'One can't believe impossible things.' I daresay
you 'haven't had much practice,' said the Queen.
'When I was your age, I always did it for half-an-hour
a day. Why, sometimes I've believed as many
as six impossible things before breakfast."

Lewis Carroll

Introduction

The British East India Company received a Royal Charter from Queen Elizabeth I in 1600. Two years later, Holland followed with the Dutch East India Company. These are among the earliest multinational enterprises (MNEs). In 1670, The Hudson Bay Company was incorporated by English royal charter as The Governor and Company of Adventurers of England trading into the Hudson's Bay. It functioned as the *de facto* government in parts of North America. Today, with headquarters in Toronto, it owns retail stores in Canada, Germany, Belgium and the US, including Lord and Taylor and Saks Fifth Avenue.

Both East India companies were trading companies with political and military interests in Southeast Asia. Items produced, acquired and traded included cotton, indigo dye, opium, salt, saltpetre, spices and tea. Their interaction with local society is a topic of continuing controversy. The television series "The Jewel in the Crown", and books *Passage to India* and Ferdinand Mount's *The Tears of the Rajahs* (2015), perhaps give a more vivid description of events on the Indian subcontinent than those of economic historians.

The local populations did not always appreciate the presence of foreigners, both those with commercial interests and others. In response to a rebellious act in 1857 in India, a British General drove the rebels into subjection by blasting 40 live mutineers out of the mouths of loaded cannons. Actions like these tended to give the foreigner a bad name, and coloured the conduct of the commercial interests which the military was there to protect. MNEs have always had a mixed report card, at least publicly, and continue to be studied by a variety of disciplines aside from economists.

Today, 400 hundred years later, the names of major companies with international dimensions include Apple, Facebook, Google, Uber and, for a while, Blackberry. All do business internationally, but often in a way far different from those like Ford, GE, IBM and Standard Oil, around which much of economic and business literature on MNEs has evolved from the 1960s. Canada has had its own batch of international players, including Alcan, Inco, Massey Ferguson and the banks. The turnover of large firms is more rapid today. In 1958, companies remained listed in the S&P 500 index for an average of 61 years, in 2013 for 18.

The challenge for economists is to concoct theories which explain the existence and impact of MNEs at particular times and as circumstances change. For me, Carleton turned out to be a fertile place to study these issues. Home to a bunch of "foxy" economists who took part in the analysis and debates, it was good to have as colleagues Keith Acheson, Al Litvak, Don McFetridge, John McManus and Gilles Paquet, amongst others.

Globalization since around 1970

The literature on MNEs evolved as changing technology affected the production and distribution of goods and services. From the 1970s, an emerging era of new technology led to the current conditions labeled "globalization". Existing MNEs have had to adapt or go out of business as in the case of Kodak, NTL and Blackberry.

Consider some of the technologies that have brought us to today, such as freight containers, ships and ports; jet planes used for passengers and freight; communications satellites; and mutual funds along with other techniques of financing. The use of shipping containers dates from the Korean War in the 1950s when they were used to transport military goods. A US manufacturer then decided that the contents of a freight truck could be separated from the means of transportation, and the container became a way of moving goods by truck, train, ship and plane – similar in many ways to the difference between content and carriage in communication industries. Container ships and ports evolved from this development, allowing both intermediate and final goods to be shipped internationally, thus influencing the location, sourcing and marketing decisions of MNEs.

The jet engine and plane date from the end of World War II, and have since been used for the transportation of both goods and people. A firm like Fedex owns its own fleet of planes, providing sourcing and delivery services for MNEs with operations around the world, especially for lightweight items. Other firms using air transport are UPS and Amazon, either owning or leasing planes. These services give firms options as to where to source and locate globally. Amazon is experimenting with drone delivery of packages. Drones may become used by those wanting to move goods and people over physical distances, and over tariff and other walls built between countries.

Communications satellites date from 1957 with Sputnik 1. Today they provide instant communication services for MNEs, as well as for terrorists, to administer their global operations. In a sense, they are the nervous system of these firms. Some MNEs specialize in communications services and provide these services to others.

None of this commercial activity would have been possible without the evolution of financial institutions. Not only did banks become global, but contracts, like mutual funds, were developed to collect and disburse funds internationally. Medical analogies are often helpful in understanding the organizational structures and flows within multinational organizations. When something goes right or screws up in a commercial firm, there is often a medical parallel which throws light on the problem.

Over time, international investment has grown along with trade and the emergence of MNEs. The 2016 *World Investment Report* shows the stock of foreign direct investment rose from $2tr in 1990 to $25tr in 2015 in current dollars, and now stands at about one-third of world GDP. Sales of foreign affiliates are also growing both absolutely and as a percentage of export sales, from 21 percent of world GDP in 1990 to 46 percent in 2013.

Globalization and the future

Forecasting is a dangerous pastime and economists don't excel at it. Who, for example, would have predicted current global economic and political conditions ten, five or even two years ago? How might globalization affect industries in the future and how will MNEs adapt? A glimpse into the future requires looking at the ways globalization is affecting production processes in a whole range of industries: resource-based, manufacturing and services. These are issues which students of economics and business will have to address by developing theoretical insights and undertaking empirical research.

The following are a few of the possibilities that may be worth monitoring: hydroponic growth of fruits and vegetables, renewable energy, 3-D printing technology, videoconferencing, and LED lighting. Some of these suggest that international production can be drawn back and become entirely or at least more localized. MNEs won't disappear, but there will be changes to both their structure and strategy. Those that fail to adapt, as occurred with Kodak, will likely face extinction. Those that exploit these technologies may flourish.

Some industries and sectors may be largely unaffected by change. Hairdressers, undertakers, caregivers, security and cleaning firms provide services which are delivered close to the customer. International franchise arrangements may influence their organization, as has been the case in the spread of fast food and beverage outlets. The Uberization of economic activities is another organizational development to watch as firms have to make use of underutilized resources.

Theories of FDI and MNEs

From around the 1960s, economists began to develop theories of the reasons for and effects of foreign direct investment (FDI) and MNEs. Early scholars include Richard Caves (1971), John Dunning (1958), Stephen Hymer (1960), Charles Kindleberger (1969), John McManus (1971), and Raymond Vernon (1968). The list is lengthy. Specialized topics such as transfer pricing were and continue to be the focus of economists like Lorraine Eden (1988).

The topic became a subject of interest not only to economists and business professors but to political scientists, lawyers and sociologists. Carleton faculty were involved in these early years with a volume edited by Gilles Paquet (1972), containing articles by Paquet, Al Litvak, Christopher Maule and John McManus.

Some early examples of FDI were related to the inputs needed for both raw materials and manufactured items such as clothing, and nutrition. Later on, investment took place to gain access to raw materials, including bauxite, copper and oil. Inputs located in one place were, and still are, often processed and distributed elsewhere. Aside from Canadian-based MNEs, more numerous American, European and some Japanese firms evolved in manufacturing industries, including petroleum refining, automobiles, pharmaceuticals, food products, as well as in services such as banking, insurance and communications.

Firms, structured to take advantage of the technology prevailing for these industries, aimed at the reduction of both transaction and processing costs. Various degrees of vertical integration occurred. This is now called supply chain management, which deals with many of the same issues in the context of current means of production.

Analytical approaches

Past theories of FDI emphasized investment along with the structure and strategy of MNEs. Investment was often a choice between trade and investment. If firms were unable to sell into a market because of trade barriers, then there existed an incentive to hop the border and locate production there, discussed as the miniature replica effect in Canada.

Other firms located abroad in order to gain access to lower cost labour than could be found at home. But this too gave rise to alternatives such as importing labour either as temporary foreign workers or as immigrants. The interacting influence of trade, investment and migration shaped the way that firms structured their worldwide operations, as well as the domestic and foreign policies that influenced these decisions.

Once the focus is placed on these three flows, then the effect of domestic policies and international agreements, including measures affecting intellectual property, come into play. Not that these have been ignored in previous research, but contemporary policy initiatives need to be integrated into future analytical work.

For example, the World Trade Organization (WTO) exists alongside numerous bilateral and regional trade, investment and intellectual property agreements, the Trans Pacific Partnership (TPP) being one current example. The WTO has received over 600 notifications of regional trade agreements. Brexit is another example of a political decision that will shake up the factors affecting trade and investment.

John Weekes (2016), Canada's chief negotiator for NAFTA and ambassador to the WTO, has written about the importance of the Trans Pacific Partnership agreement for Canada, even if the US does not ratify it. He notes that foreign sales of Canadian foreign affiliates are now about 30 percent of Canadian GDP. The final ratification of the Canada-Europe Free Trade Agreement (CETA) is another example of what may be in the mill for investment as well as trade.

Policy dimension

How have policies towards MNEs and FDI evolved? Canada has long provided input into the debate and the nationalistic discourse. In 1930, Ken W. Taylor, then a professor of economics at McMaster University, and later to become a Deputy Minister of Finance and ex-officio director of the Bank of Canada, estimated about $4bn of American investment in Canada at that time. The numbers may have included portfolio investment.

In the 1960s, Canadian nationalistic pressures grew to do something about foreign investment. The Liberal government of Lester Pearson, with Walter Gordon as Finance Minister, appointed Mel Watkins to chair the Task Force on Ownership and the Structure of Canadian Industry (1968). Two more government reports were followed by the formation of the Foreign Investment Review Agency in 1973, now Investment Canada. Harry Johnson and numerous Canadian academics were and continue to be engaged in examining these issues.

A challenge for economists has been to isolate a theory of the multinational enterprise from the mass of transactions that are undertaken internationally. There are theories of portfolio and direct investment, of international trade in goods and of the international movement of persons and services like intellectual property, all of which are somehow related to MNEs, but don't necessarily explain what some MNE literature is trying to get at. But then there are other concerns which muddy the analysis.

The motivation of some writers stems from the MNE being seen as a means to transfer power, so that one state can influence political decision-making in another. Investment by an MNE owned in a developed country may be able to influence political decision-making in a developing country, where valuable natural resources are found, thereby creating an actual or potential loss of political independence. For example, Canada is today concerned about foreign investment from countries like Russia and China, and was more so during the Cold War. But historically most of the Canadian unease has been about investment from the US. How has this played out in Canada?

The public discourse can be found in the work of Kari Levitt, *Silent Surrender: The Multinational Corporation in Canada* (1970), and in the formation of the Council of Canadians in 1985, at the time of the negotiations for the Canada-US Free Trade Agreement. The majority of economists saw FDI as an efficient means to transfer capital and knowledge for the economic benefit of both capital exporting and importing countries. Many political scientists and others thought otherwise.

Conclusion

So where does all this leave economists today ploughing in the fields of foreign investment and MNEs? A wide range of conditions and policies in both the capital exporting and importing countries need to be considered. For example, a firm may invest abroad to gain access to low cost foreign labour. Alternatively, labour may be imported by way of immigration or temporary foreign workers, as occurs with Caribbean farm workers in Canada and Polish plumbers in the UK. The political dimension was front and centre in the US 2016 presidential election, where an estimated 11 million illegal foreign workers were an issue; one estimate for Canada is 500,000 but no one knows because illegals don't offer themselves up to be counted.

Investment deals with an economic transaction while the enterprise focuses on the way these transactions are organized. The two are difficult to separate. The legal form of the transaction varies according to a set of prevailing economic incentives affecting different forms of investment, trade in goods, trade in services, including intellectual property, and the movement of labour. Each situation is different. Thus the existence of

MNEs and the forms they take will depend on things like tariffs, controls on investment, the movement of labour, either as migrants or as temporary foreign workers, as well as the perceived political risk of investing in a foreign jurisdiction.

Commercial decisions that investors make for the domestic market only are, in general, similar to those made when foreign investment takes place. It is just that things like commercial and currency risks may vary as well as other costs of production. A knowledge of trade agreements, both those in force and those under negotiation, matter for the investor, as well as for those academics trying to craft theories of the MNE. The underlying economic factors affecting decision making for the domestic market are similar to those for the foreign investor. Differences arise because trading and investing abroad give rise to additional factors such as political risk.

The opening quote from Lewis Carroll captures the researcher's challenges and opportunities, a need to think the impossible in developing hypotheses and looking for ways to test them. A starting point for me and many others is the work of Nobel Laureate Ronald Coase with his article, "The Nature of the Firm" (1937). It is discussed by the author in the April 2003 Centennial Coase Lecture at the University of Chicago (available at http://www.law.uchicago.edu/video/coase040103). This provides one access point today for anyone entering this field of study.

Christopher Maule was a member of Carleton's Economics Department from 1962 to 1964 and from 1970 to 1995, when he retired from full-time teaching. From 1988 to 1993, he was Director of the Norman Paterson School of International Affairs, during which time a greater emphasis was placed on economics. His research, much of it co-authored with Carleton colleagues Keith Acheson and Al Litvak, emphasized the role of multinational corporations in the context of international trade, investment and migration, and on the political economy of the cultural industries. Since 2000, he has written a blog dealing with a range of topics, many of which have an economic dimension. His blog is found at cmaule.wordpress.com.

References

Caves, Richard. 1971. "International Corporations: The Industrial Economics of Foreign Investment," *Economica*, vol. 28, p. 1-27.

Coase, Ronald. 1937. "The Nature of the Firm," *Economica*, 4(16): 386-405.

Dunning, John. 1958. *American Investment in British Manufacturing Industry*. London, UK: Allen and Unwin.

Eden, Lorraine. 1988. "Equity and neutrality in the multinational taxation of capital," *Osgoode Hall Law Journal*, vol. 26, p. 367-408.

Hymer, Stephen. 1960. "International Operations of National Firms – A Study of Direct Foreign Investment," Ph.D. Dissertation. Cambridge, MA: MIT.

Kindleberger, Charles. 1969. *American Investment Abroad: Six Lectures on Direct Investment*. New Haven, CN: Yale University Press.

McManus, John. 1971. "The Organization of Production," Ph.D. Dissertation. Toronto, ON.

Paquet, Gilles (ed.). 1972. *The Multinational Firm and the Nation State*. Toronto, ON: Collier-Macmillan.

Vernon, Raymond (ed.). 1968. *Multinational Enterprises in the 1960s*. London, UK: Royal Institute of International Affairs.

Weekes, John. 2016. "Choices for the Future: the Trans-Pacific Partnership and Canada," Calgary, AB: Canadian Global Affairs Institute, http://www.cgai.ca/choices_for_the_future_the_tpp_and_canada.

PART III.
Money and Finance

Out of the Ivory Tower

By Georg Rich

On a recent trip to Jena, Germany, I visited a museum operated by the Carl-Zeiss Company, the well-known producer of microscopes and other optical instruments. I was greatly impressed by the story of Carl Zeiss, the founder of the company. Zeiss was a gifted optician and lens maker, whose designs of microscopes were considered to range among the best at that time. By trial and error, he managed gradually to improve the quality of lenses built into his microscopes. However, towards the end of the 1860s, Zeiss, to his great dismay, realized that as a practitioner, and even as a highly-skilled one, he was running up against a dead end. Despite his relentless tinkering, his optical instruments left much to be desired. If he was to produce better lenses, he had to embark on a new approach. It dawned on him that he needed a theory in order to achieve his ambition of triggering a quantum leap in the manufacturing of lenses.

For this reason, in 1872 he approached Ernst Abbe, an underpaid physics professor at the University of Jena, who agreed to cooperate with Zeiss, as he was desperate for extra money to support his family. Working on Zeiss's problem, Abbe made a path-breaking discovery, the so-called "Abbe sine condition". This condition must be satisfied if a lens or other optical system is to generate sharp images. Unfortunately, the Abbe formula, by itself, did not allow Zeiss to design better lenses. It required a particularly strong form of glass that was unavailable at that time. Therefore, Abbe teamed up with Otto Schott, a glass chemist, who was able to produce the required type of glass. The successful interplay of theory and practice lead to the quantum leap envisaged by Zeiss. Thanks to Abbe's discovery, the Carl-Zeiss company became and remained for a long time the leading manufacturer of optical instruments.

Although optics and economics have little in common, the Zeiss-Abbe story, in my view, conveys an important message to our profession. Although the combination of theory and practice may produce important results, there exists, unfortunately too often, a considerable gap between the researchers working in the ivory towers of universities and the human beings trying to cope with real-world economic issues, whom, for simplicity, I will call the "practitioners". The practitioners frequently complain that researchers have become too theoretical and mathematical, with the results of high-tech academic research appearing to be of little relevance to them. Researchers, by contrast, scold practitioners for their inability to dissect adequately economic issues and to fall for simplistic solutions to complex economic problems. However, fruitful cooperation between researchers and practitioners is important if we are to find adequate solutions to the world's burning economic problems. Monetary policy is a good case in point.

After Carleton

After I had left Carleton University and academe in 1977, I joined the research department of the Swiss National Bank (SNB), Switzerland's central bank, and became deeply involved in monetary policy for the subsequent 24 years. The SNB had just established a research department that was to support the Board, the SNB's decision-making body, in setting monetary policy. Very few central banks had research departments at that time. Furthermore, the research departments actually in existence frequently did not play a significant role in the formulation of monetary policy. The SNB's aim was to make research an integral part of the policy decision-making process.

Consequently, the researchers were expected to make an important contribution to the formulation of monetary policy.

The need for research derived from the fact that Switzerland had adopted a floating exchange rate in 1973 in the wake of the collapse of the Bretton-Woods system. Since the SNB was no longer compelled to defend a fixed exchange rate, it acquired the power to gear monetary policy to domestic objectives such as price stability. At that time, inflation in Switzerland as in other countries was relatively high. The SNB was convinced that the prime objective of monetary policy was to restore price stability, a view that was shared by the Swiss government and wide segments of the Swiss public. To rein in inflation, the SNB opted for a pragmatic version of a monetarist approach, based on annual growth targets for, first, the money stock M1 and later for the monetary base. Thanks to tight control of the money supply, the SNB was able to reduce inflation to low levels relatively quickly even though it could not avoid temporary surges in inflation in subsequent years. In principle, the SNB maintained this policy approach until 1999, when it switched to a concept resembling inflation targeting. The SNB's Board realized that sensible targets for money growth could not be set without research providing the required input into the decision-making process.

When I joined the SNB, I thought that I was well prepared for my new job. At Carleton University, I had taught money, banking and international finance besides other subjects. Moreover, I had been involved in research in the monetary area. However, after I had descended from the heights of the ivory tower to the lows of practical monetary policy, I encountered new challenges that had not caused me any pains in academe.

Two challenges were particularly noteworthy.

First, the task of the researchers was to come up with precise policy proposals for charting the SNB's policy course, proposals that could actually be implemented by the staff members dealing in the money and foreign exchange markets. Such proposals could not simply be extracted from economic textbooks or papers in scientific journals. Coming up with sensible proposals not only required knowledge of economic analysis and research tailored to the specific policy situation, but also a good feel for what was happening in the economies in Switzerland and the rest of the world.

Second, the researchers had to be able to communicate their policy proposals to the Board, whose members were not always well versed in economic analysis, as well as to the staff dealing in the money and foreign exchange markets. In addition, we were responsible for drafting press releases communicating our policy decisions to the public, as well as for drafting and delivering speeches explaining our monetary policy to the public. Since the SNB was among the first central banks shredding the veil of secrecy that had traditionally surrounded monetary policy, it attached a great deal of importance to a constructive dialogue with the press and the public.

Two examples of these challenges

Focus on price stability

A problem encountered by all central banks is that the public frequently expects too much from monetary policy. Central banks should guarantee stable prices, moderate the business cycle, help governments finance their budget deficits, and provide for an adequate exchange rate, and orderly conditions in the banking system and financial markets. Achieving simultaneously stability of prices and output is particularly tricky. According to past experience, central banks that, depending on the state of the economy, are prone to switch from inflation to output objectives or *vice versa* tend to enhance, rather than mitigate, economic stability. Fine tuning the business cycle almost always turns out to be an exercise in futility. For this reason, the SNB emphasized that monetary policy should be employed mainly to achieve price stability. However, the focus on price stability did not imply that the central bank ignored output and the business cycle. Even though it did not endeavour to stabilize output, it had to monitor the output gap, which tends to be an important leading indicator of future inflation. Furthermore, the SNB always stressed that achieving price stability meant warding off inflation *and deflation*. In a recession, prices were under downward pressure, prompting the central bank to switch to an expansionary monetary policy. In this way, it contributed both to maintaining price stability and stabilizing output. In a boom period, by contrast, the central bank was forced to tighten monetary policy in an effort to preserve price stability. This also served to curb growth in output. A real conflict between price and output stability only arose in the case of cost-push inflation, triggered, for example, by a hike in the oil price, leading both to an increase in the general price level and a fall in output. Considering shocks on the cost side, the SNB stressed that it would not attempt to reverse the initial price increase, but would ensure that the cost-push would not generate a long-lasting acceleration of inflation.

As we gained experience with monetary targeting, we discovered various flaws in the monetarist approach. Our main problem, at least until the late 1990s, was not so much instability in money demand, which undermined monetary targeting in various other countries, including Canada. Rather, steady money growth, as demanded by the monetarist approach, turned out to be an inadequate stabilizer of cyclical fluctuations in inflation and output. Monetarists, in general, believed that a cyclical expansion (contraction) in economic activity would trigger an increase (decrease) in interest rates provided the central bank augmented the money supply at a steady pace. The increase (decrease) in interest rates, in turn, would help to curb the cyclical fluctuations in inflation and output. However, in Switzerland, money demand was quite sensitive to movements in interest rates, implying that steady money growth would elicit only modest pro-cyclical changes in interest rates, which were not potent enough to act as an effective stabilizer of inflation and output.[1] This flaw, coupled with rising instability in money demand, prompted the SNB to abandon monetary targeting in the late 1990s. Nevertheless, monetary targeting enabled the SNB to reduce the trend in inflation to low levels, lower than

---

[1] In a critical review of monetarism, Benjamin M. Friedman (1977) had already pointed to this potential flaw.

in most other countries, despite the occasional cyclical surge in the inflation rate.

Although explaining the SNB's policy approach to the public was quite a challenge, the public, on the whole, understood that monetary policy could not be all things to all people. It generally accepted the focus on price stability. Of course, there were critics claiming that the SNB, had it the courage to replace the pigheaded monetarists by truly imaginative economists, could easily manage to fine tune the business cycle, stabilize the exchange rate and achieve price stability. But the public, in general, was satisfied with the SNB's policy approach and its performance.

Exchange rate intervention

Soon after Switzerland had adopted a floating exchange rate, the SNB, from time to time, began to encounter excessive up valuations of the Swiss franc that were at variance with economic fundamentals, and threatened to undermine the competitive position of Swiss industry on world markets. These leaps in the exchange rate posed a dilemma for the SNB. In setting its monetary targets, the SNB, of course, took account of the exchange rate, besides other factors. The SNB could not go as far as trying to meet a specific target for the exchange rate. This would have implied a *de facto* return to a fixed exchange rate, with the attendant loss of control over the money supply and inflation. Even a temporary exchange rate peg would have compelled the SNB to intervene on the foreign exchange market. As it acquired foreign exchange in an effort to halt an excessive appreciation of the Swiss franc, it could not help expanding the money supply since it had to purchase the foreign currencies by issuing domestic money. Depending on the economic environment, the expansion in the money supply might have been inconsistent with preserving price stability in the longer run.

One could argue that the SNB could have escaped from this dilemma by conducting sterilized interventions, i.e., by siphoning off the excess money through sales of domestic bonds to the public. In this way, the SNB would have balanced the purchases of foreign exchange by reducing its holdings of domestic bonds. However, standard macroeconomic models suggest that sterilized interventions are ineffective in influencing the exchange rate if capital is perfectly mobile internationally. In the Swiss case, the assumption of perfect capital mobility is certainly valid. Consequently, it is hardly surprising that the SNB never found sterilized interventions to be effective and seldom used this instrument.[2] This implies that the dilemma described above is real.

Occasionally, the jumps in the exchange rate were so large that the SNB had to react. In 1978 a huge appreciation of the Swiss franc threatened to plunge the Swiss economy into a serious recession. The Board asked the staff to come up with a solution to the problem and we suggested fixing a temporary exchange rate target. The Board accepted the proposal and set a temporary floor under the Swiss franc price of the Deutsche mark. As a result, the SNB was forced to buy massive amounts of foreign exchange and to accept a large-scale increase in the money supply. In this way, the SNB managed to calm the turmoil in the foreign exchange market. Although it returned to strict monetary targeting after a few months, it could not avoid a renewed surge in inflation, which, in all likelihood, was due to the fact that we overestimated the effectiveness of the monetary target as a cyclical stabilizer.

Conclusions

What conclusions can be drawn from these examples? Clearly, close cooperation between researchers and practitioners is necessary if we are to come up with sensible solutions to

[2] Various empirical studies on sterilized interventions have uncovered statistically significant effects on the exchange rate, stressing announcement effects and other factors as possible reasons for this result. Since such studies tend to be based on high-frequency data, it is unclear whether these effects are long lasting or tend to prevail only for a few days or hours. Considering the Swiss experience, I am convinced that sterilized interventions are useless in an environment of perfect capital mobility.

economic problems. We need more researchers, especially the best in their fields, willing occasionally to descend from the ivory tower and to apply their analytical tools to trying to solve the economic problems bothering the practitioners. By the same token, the practitioners should listen to the researchers and endeavour to understand their analysis. This leads us to the theme of this volume. What does the call for closer cooperation between researchers and practitioners mean for the future of economics, in particular, for my field of monetary economics? In my view, my field does not suffer from an excess of mathematics and high-tech research. Rather, I would like to see greater willingness by researchers to address the concerns of practitioners. Universities could make a contribution by filling their frequently sterile macroeconomics courses with real life, allowing students to better comprehend how they can apply in practice the analytical tools they have acquired. In this way, the students would get a flavour of what will await them once they leave the ivory tower.

Georg Rich taught economics at Carleton from 1967 to 1977, and served as chairman of Carleton's Economics Department from 1972 to 1974. He joined the Swiss National Bank in 1977 and was appointed chief economist in 1985. After his retirement from the SNB in 2001, he became an honorary professor at the University of Bern, and also taught a course at the Graduate Institute of International and Development Studies in Geneva. He has published widely on monetary matters, including studies on the Eurocurrency markets, Canadian monetary history and Swiss monetary policy.

References

Friedman, Benjamin M. 1977. "The inefficiency of short-run monetary targets for monetary policy," *Brookings Papers on Economic Activity*, vol. 2, p. 293-346.

Financial Institutions in Canada

By John Chant

When I first started teaching in the early 1960s, the financial industry was on the brink of a massive transformation and today bears slight resemblance to what it was then. The story is not one of steady evolution. Change was kick-started first by the monumental 1964 *Report of the Royal Commission on Banking and Finance* (the Porter Commission) (Canada 1964) and the resulting 1970 *Bank Act*. Financial failures in the early 1980s and, more recently, the banking crisis of 2008 have spurred further change, while innovation has started to reshape the payments sector.

Regulation and financial structure

One force driving change in the financial industry has been periodic revisions of legislation mandated by built-in sunset clauses. Much of the legislative change from this source has been directed toward the Porter Commission's goals of competition and efficiency.

In the early 1960s, Canada's financial industry was structured around four separate pillars. Two of the pillars consisted of deposit-taking institutions: chartered banks in one pillar, and trust and mortgage loan companies in the other. The other two pillars were composed of investment dealers and life insurers. Credit unions/*caisses populaires* made up a possible fifth pillar.

The pillars hardly overlapped, making competition between them slight. Though banks and trust and loan companies both accepted funds from the general public, they were restricted in the uses to which they could put the funds. Banks could lend through commercial loans and only those mortgages that were government insured; trust and loan companies were virtually confined to mortgages. Banking was the dominant pillar in terms of size and had become concentrated over the years through numerous mergers, leaving just five major banks.

The first crack in the pillars appeared when the *Bank Act* of 1967 allowed banks to lend through conventional mortgages. The trust and loan companies at the time were ill-equipped to deal with the challenge of greater competition because, as short-term borrowers and long-term lenders, they had their financial condition weakened by the high interest rates of the 1970s that pushed up their cost of funds. The crumbling continued when banks started acquiring trust companies once permitted by the 1992 *Bank Act*, blending this business with their own. Now the banks have absorbed the major trust and loan companies and the sector is a shadow of its former self.

A similar collapse took place in the investment industry pillar. Banks increasingly saw the investment industry's underwriting as a threat to their corporate loan business. Four large banks then moved in 1987 to buy the major investment dealers, despite the securities business being under provincial jurisdiction.

As it happened, the easing of the boundaries between the banking and investment industry pillars had mixed effects. The added clout of the banks in the security business was offset by the removal of competitors from the marketplace.

Competition in the deposit-taking industry was also diminished when Canada's open approach to foreign banks was challenged in 1965 by a large US bank's proposal to buy a small bank that was already foreign owned (Fayerweather 1974). The thought of such a large US bank coming to Canada provoked the Minister of Finance to strongly oppose the take-over, leading to the government curtailing further foreign bank activity by imposing a 10 percent limit on bank ownership by a single party and a 25 percent limit on foreign ownership in the 1967 *Bank Act*. Despite the limits, foreign banks continued to operate in Canada through agents, representative offices and non-bank financial companies much to the dismay of the Canadian banking community. The 1980 *Bank Act* met these concerns by allowing for a tightly controlled entry by foreign banks through subsidiaries with strict limits on the size of each bank, the number of branches and the total size of foreign banks overall, with all foreign banking activities conducted through the subsidiaries. Subsequent bank acts have eased the limits on the foreign banks' subsidiaries and allowed foreign bank branches to operate with lending powers and some with limited deposit-taking powers. Foreign banks now account for 3 percent of total bank assets through their subsidiaries and branches.

The fifth pillar, credit unions and *caisses populaires,* has been able to increase its role as a result of a number of regulatory changes. Provinces eased the requirement of a common bond among members in terms of religion, occupation, employer or place of residence, giving credit union locals the opportunity to grow to a more efficient scale, often through mergers. Revisions of the federal legislation have further eased constraints on the organization of credit unions by allowing union centrals to operate across provinces in 2002 and by giving the same powers to credit union locals in 2014.

The credit union/*caisses* system has also been strengthened by the expansion of depositor protection from provincial governments, in some cases without any limit. Deposit insurance is at once both a blessing and a curse. It is a blessing in that it stabilizes an institution's funding, avoiding disastrous runs on deposits of the past. It is a curse by encouraging institutions to piggyback on the protection and take greater risks. It is troubling that the highest rates on term deposits are offered by credit union locals covered by 100 percent government guarantees.[1]

[1] https://www.cannex.com/index.php/services/canada/banking-products/gics-term-deposits/

The structure of the Canadian financial system and the activities of institutions are unrecognizable from the perspective of the 1960s. Two of the three pillars have crumbled and all but disappeared. Credit unions/*caisses populaires* have increased their share of deposit-taking industry from 9 percent in 1964 to 13 percent in 2015. Over the same period, the banks have substantially increased their dominance in the sector from 70 to 86 percent.

What of the future? Is further concentration of financial activity in banks possible or desirable? In 1998, the Minister of Finance turned down several proposed mergers between chartered banks on the grounds that they would lead to an unacceptable concentration of economic power; this would result in a significant reduction of competition; and this would reduce the government's flexibility to deal with future prudential concerns.[2] Such mergers may even be less desirable now because the safety and soundness concerns expressed at the time have been magnified by the experience of the banking crisis.

Further consolidation could be possible through blending the banking and insurance pillars. Still a merger between a bank and an insurance company would pose problems for regulators. The nature of banking currently constrains banks from excessive taking by their need to retain short-term funding, a discipline that would be weakened if they had access to the pool of long-term funds that now finances the life insurance business (Calomiris and Kahn 1991). A new regulatory framework would be required to govern the risks raised by the bank-assurance business.

The evolving payment system

Prior to the 1960s, Canadians wrote cheques as the alternative to cash for making payments. The Canadian Banker's Association

---

[2] Statement by the Honourable Paul Martin, Minister of Finance, on the Bank Merger Proposals, Ottawa, December 18, 1998, 1998-124, accessed at http://www.collectionscanada.gc.ca/webarchives/20071122063125/http://www.fin.gc.ca/news98/98-124e.html.

(now Payments Canada) had operated the core clearing and settlement arrangements for cheques since 1900 and limited direct access to its members (Canada 1997). Non-bank financial institutions wishing to offer cheques to their customers could only gain access to the system through a chartered bank. Since then the payments landscape has been changed by both new payments technologies and new governance arrangements.

The first challenge to the existing system came when banks offered Visa credit cards to their customers in 1968 and MasterCard credit cards in 1973. While some users rely on the credit services of the cards, many use them as pure payments cards by paying their balance monthly. Notably, credit cards bypass the cheque payments system to pay merchants and to collect from consumers directly.

A further payment innovation occurred in 1994 when Interac Association introduced its national debit card service. Unlike credit cards, debit cards are pure payment cards through which consumers pay directly from their bank accounts.

The use of cards has substantially changed Canadians' payment methods. The number of cheques passing through Payments Canada has fallen steadily from over 1.5 billion per year in the mid-1990s to 650 million in 2015 and makes up just 5 percent of non-cash payments. Credit and debit cards, in contrast, are used for 9.2 billion transactions or 76 percent of non-cash transactions (Bank for International Settlements).

On the governance side, the Porter Commission recognized that the Bankers' Association's hold on the core of the payments system placed other financial institutions at a disadvantage and recommended setting up an association open to all financial institutions to manage the system. Implementation followed only in 1980 when the clearing and settlement system was assigned the Canadian Payments Association, an independent body. Directors without affiliation to financial institutions were added to the Association's board in 2002 and became a majority of the board in 2014.

The Canadian payment system has fallen behind others in adopting new technologies as some countries have eliminated paper transactions entirely. Moving forward to replace cheques with digital payments would save businesses, at a rough estimate, some $1.6 to $4.4 billion a year (Chant 2015).

The payments industry, essentially an information industry that keeps track of transactions between payers and recipients, can benefit like other information industries from advances in technology. Already, the credit card industry has embraced digital technology and high-tech businesses, including Apple, Google and Microsoft. Together with many small businesses, they are creating new ways for making payments: some will build on existing payments to make them more efficient and others will provide substitutes that displace them. Some countries are even experimenting with digital alternatives to currency and coin while Bitcoin, Ethereum and other crypto-currencies are innovative payments systems that could bypass national currencies (Andofatto 2014).

Payments Canada continues to hold a monopoly over interbank payments, including large value transfers that have average value of over $5.3 million. Will the growth of competing payment systems, both domestic and international, weaken the monopoly and limit the ability of the Bank of Canada and other authorities to maintain the stability of the payments so vital to the Canadian economy? Does this monopoly, on the other hand, stifle the innovation necessary for an efficient payment system?

The regulatory response to financial sector developments

Policy makers' responses to developments taking place in the financial industry are another factor driving change. The responsibility for regulating deposit-taking institutions was predominantly federal in the 1960s. At the time its regulation was minimal and could be best described as "hands off". The Office of the Inspector-General of Banks, the bank regulator, had only a small staff and relied on the reports of the banks' external auditors. Despite this limited oversight and the absence of deposit insurance, Canadian banks appear to have survived the Great Depression with little damage (Roberts and Kryzanowski 1993).[3] Unlike the US, Canada did not have deposit insurance.

A period of relative calm was broken up by the failure of Atlantic Acceptance in 1965 just before the report of the Porter Commission which expressed the view that deposit insurance was not needed (Canada 1964: 282). Nevertheless, the federal government reacted by establishing the Canada Deposit Insurance Corporation in 1967, with coverage of $20,000 per deposit. Ontario and Quebec also introduced deposit insurance for their deposit-taking institutions.

Canada's approach to regulation was challenged when a series of failures of financial institutions swept through the financial system from the early 1980s through the 1990s. The costs of the failures exhausted CDIC's resources and forced it to turn for aid to the federal government. In the aftermath, the government established the Office of the Superintendent of Financial Institutions (OSFI) in 1987 in a move toward a more hands on approach to regulation. OSFI now regularly audits financial institutions and makes use of its regulatory powers to influence their conduct.[4]

When the Canadian financial sector was side-swiped by the 2007-08 US financial crisis, Canadian authorities took extraordinary measures to prevent its spread (Chant 2014). The Bank of Canada made credit easier through larger and more frequent purchase-and-resale agreements, through the creation of longer-term credit facilities, and through a broadening of acceptable collateral. The government itself offered guarantees for new debt issues by financial institutions and provided for purchase of up to $75 billion of insured mortgages by the Canada Mortgage and Housing Corporation.

---

[3] Roberts and Kryzanowski suggest that Canadian banks may have been technically bankrupt during part of the 1930s but were saved from failure by the authority's forbearance. See Roberts and Kryzanowski (1993).

[4] See Chapter 5: "Regulating and Supervision of Large Banks" in the *2010 Fall Report of the Auditor General of Canada*, accessed at http://www.oag-bvg.gc.ca/internet/English/parl_oag_201010_e_34282.html.

These initiatives dwarfed any previous measures taken to support our banks. Still we experienced a smaller impact of the crisis on our banks and the rest of our financial system than most other countries, earning many plaudits for the soundness of the Canadian banking system.

Today, the most troubling question is whether the policy responses to the 2008 financial crisis have been sufficient. This may not appear to be a Canadian concern since our financial institutions stood up well, but each crisis is different and we may not be so lucky next time. Despite much progress to overcome the weaknesses exposed by the financial crisis, there remains work to be done.

And for the future

The problems posed by potential financial crises can be dealt with either through prevention or cure. Prevention means making financial institutions "too safe to fail" while cure means ensuring that if they do fail, they "fail safely". While progress has been made on both fronts, too much attention has been placed on failing safely. Major Canadian financial institutions are huge with some having assets as large as 70 percent of GDP, together with complex financial structures and myriad obligations owing from and due to counterparties throughout the world that would be tough to unwind. Fail-safe procedures give no chance for a trial run.

Some suggest as a preventative measure raising capital requirements to make financial institutions too safe to fail.[5] Canada's chief regulator concedes that, despite progress since the crisis, room still remains for further improvement (Rudin 2016). While International Monetary Fund economists suggest that capital levels of 15 to 23 percent would have been sufficient in a large proportion of banking crises and that benefits decline rapidly beyond this level, they admit that such levels would not

---

[5] Capital requirements refer to the total of various measures of the shareholders' stake in an institution relative to its assets. Capital acts as a buffer that protects depositors by bearing the first costs of decreases in the value of an institution's assets.

be sufficient for more extreme crises (Dagher *et al.* 2016). Other economists suggest even higher levels of bank capital: Admati and Helwig propose a return to the past capital levels of 20 to 30 percent of bank funding (Admati and Helwig 2013).

There are economists who argue for more radical measures. A former Governor of the Bank of England paints banking as a fragile alchemy that works well in normal times, but is at risk of falling apart (King 2015). He proposes that banks become "narrow banks" and hold only safe, liquid assets so that they can always meet their customers' demands for withdrawals. In doing so, he is following the lead of Milton Friedman and James Tobin, two Nobel Prize winners from opposite ends of the political spectrum (Chant 1995).

Attempts to strengthen regulated institutions by higher capital requirements or conversion to narrow banks may push their traditional activities out to the so-called grey market where financial enterprises operate outside the scope of regulation. If this happens, such a move, rather than solving the problem of crises, just shifts it to another place. Though the grey market institutions lie beyond the scope of regulation, governments would find it difficult to resist pressure to rescue them if they were threatened by a crisis.

So-called Fintec enterprises pose similar problems as the grey market. These businesses use innovative information technologies to offer new financial services and new ways of accessing traditional services. Some activities, such as lending financed through equity capital, do not require prudential regulation. However, any activity that collects and holds deposit-like funds from the general public should be subject to regulation.

Both the grey market and Fintec firms highlight the need to direct regulation toward what institutions do rather than their legal status. With many of these entities operating under provincial auspices, any effort by the federal government to extend regulation may be stymied by the constitutional division of powers. The recent Supreme Court's decision offers some hope in its declaration that "management of systemic risk" is national in scope (Johnston, Rockwell and Ford 2014: 666). Unfortunately, this experience suggests the process could be long and drawn-out.

Conclusion

Today's Canadian financial sector would hardly be recognizable in the 1960s. Innovation and competition has evolved in ways that better serve the needs of Canadians. Further progress is possible, but many of the changes underway will require the rethinking of policy. Nimble responses based on the activities performed and the issues they raise can give Canadians the benefits of fast-paced innovation while maintaining a safe and stable financial system.

John Chant retired in 2002 from the Department of Economics at Simon Fraser University. He had previously taught at Carleton University from 1972 to 1979. He has written extensively on financial institutions and their regulation. Chant was a Special Adviser to the Governor of the Bank of Canada in 2001/02 and has participated in several national studies of the Canadian financial system.

References

Admati, A. and M. Hellwig. 2013. *The Bankers' New Clothes: What's Wrong with Banking and What To Do About It*. Princeton, NJ: Princeton University Press.

Andofatto, D. 2014. "Bitcoin and Beyond: The Possibilities and the Pitfalls of Virtual Currencies," presentation, March; accessed at https://www.stlouisfed.org/dialogue-with-the-fed/the-possibilities-and-the-pitfalls-of-virtual-currencies.

Auditor General of Canada. 2010. Chapter 5: "Regulating and Supervision of Large Banks," *Report of the Auditor General of Canada*; accessed at http://www.oag-bvg.gc.ca/internet/English/parl_oag_201010_e_34282.html.

Bank for International Settlements: statistics on payment, clearing and settlement systems in the CPMI countries, various issues.

Calomiris, C. and C. Kahn. 1991. "The Role of Demandable Debt in Structuring Optimal Banking Arrangements," *American Economic Review*, June, p. 497-513.

Canada. 1964. *Report of the Royal Commission on Banking and Finance (The Porter Commission)*. Ottawa, ON: Queen's Printer.

Canada. 1997. "The Payments System in Canada: An Overview of Concepts and Structures," Background paper for discussion by the Payments System Advisory Committee, Discussion Paper 1. Ottawa, ON: Bank of Canada and the Department of Finance.

Cannex: https://www.cannex.com/index.php/services/canada/banking-products/gics-term-deposits/.

Chant, J. 1995. "Canada should consider narrow banking," *Policy Options*, June, p.11-16.

Chant, J. 2014. *Keeping the Genie in the Bottle*. Calgary, AB: University of Calgary, School of Public Policy, SPP Research Papers, March.

Chant, J. 2015. *Money in Motion: Modernizing Canada's Payment System*. Ottawa, ON: C.D. Howe Institute, Commentary 432, August.

Dagher, J., G. Dell'Ariccia, L. Laeven, L. Ratnovski and H. Tong. 2016. "Benefits and Costs of Bank Capital," Staff Discussion Note, March, SDN/16/04.

Fayerweather, J. 1974. *The Mercantile Bank Affair: a case study in Canadian nationalism and a multinational firm*. New York, NY: New York University Press.

Johnston, D., K. Rockwell and C. Ford. 2014. *Canadian Securities Regulation*, Fifth Edition. North York, ON: LexisNexis Canada.

King, M. 2015. *The End of Alchemy: Money, Banking, and the Future of the Global Economy.* New York, NY: W.W. Norton & Co.

Martin, Paul. 1998. Statement by the Honourable Paul Martin, Minister of Finance, on the Bank Merger Proposals, Ottawa, December 18, p. 1998-2124; accessed at http://www. collectionscanada.gc.ca/webarchives/20071122063125/http:// www.fin.gc.ca/news98/98-124e.html.

Roberts, G. and L. Kryzanowski. 1993. "Canadian Banking Solvency, 1922-1940," *Journal of Money, Credit and Banking,* 25(3): 361-376.

Rudin, Jeremy. 2016. "The Way Forward for Bank Capital: Canada's Perspective," Remarks by the Superintendent to the Institute of International Bankers (IIB), October 25; accessed at http:/www.osfi-bsif.gc.ca.

About The Authors

John Chant retired in 2002 from the Department of Economics at Simon Fraser University. He had previously taught at Carleton University from 1972 to 1979. He has written extensively on financial institutions and their regulation. Mr. Chant was a Special Adviser to the Governor of the Bank of Canada in 2001/02 and has participated in several national studies of the Canadian financial system.

Ehsan U. Choudhri joined the Department of Economics at Carleton University in 1965. He retired from the full-time teaching position at Carleton University in 2012 and is currently a Distinguished Research Professor. He has undertaken research on a wide range of topics in international trade and macroeconomics. His has published in many journals, including *Canadian Journal of Economics*, *Journal of International Economics*, *Journal of Monetary Economics*, *Journal of Political Economy* and *Quarterly Journal of Economics*. He has held visiting positions at a number of institutions including University of California at Los Angeles, Rutgers University, Georgetown University, Bank of Canada and International Monetary Fund. He has served as chair of the Department of Economics at Carleton University and associate editor for the *Journal of International Economics*.

Steven Langdon was a member of Carleton's Economics Department from 1974 to 1984. He also taught at the Norman Paterson School of International Affairs. Then he accepted a position as Associate Director for Economics and Rural Development at the International Development Research Centre (IDRC); this followed two years on leave as IDRC Regional Program Officer for Social Sciences in Eastern and Southern Africa, based in Nairobi. His further research and project implementation has focused on poverty reduction, industrial restructuring and governance. After serving as an M.P. for nine years, he worked with the World Bank and the Parliamentary Centre in 20 different African countries as well as a number in Asia and Latin America. He is now an Adjunct Professor in the Economics Department at Carleton and is completing a textbook on African economic development for a UK publisher.

Harvey Lithwick began his teaching career a Carleton University in 1963, and served as Chairman of Carleton's Economics Department (1974-77). He was recruited by the Canadian government in 1969 to undertake a study of urban Canada and appointed Assistant Secretary to create the Ministry of State for Urban Affairs. He was a Visiting Professor at the Hebrew University in Jerusalem in 1969-70 and 1977-78. In 1992, he moved to Ben-Gurion University of the Negev in Israel where, with Professor Yehuda Gradus, he helped set up the Negev Center for Regional Development until his retirement in 2005.

Christopher Maule was a member of Carleton's Economics Department from 1962 to 1964 and from 1970 to 1995 when he retired from full-time teaching. From 1988 to 1993, he was Director of the Norman Paterson School of International Affairs during which time a greater emphasis was placed on economics. His research, much of it co-authored with Carleton colleagues Keith Acheson and Al Litvak, emphasized the role of multinational corporations in the context of international trade, investment and migration, and on the political economy of the cultural industries. Since 2000, he has written a blog dealing with a range of topics many of which have an economic dimension. His blog is found at cmaule.wordpress.com.

Donald McFetridge was a member of the Department of Economics at Carleton from 1974 until his retirement in 2013. He specialized in Industrial Organization and Competition Policy. His research efforts while at Carleton benefitted immensely from collaboration with colleagues Keith Acheson, John Chant, Ed Hughes, Douglas Smith and the late Stanley Wong, and also with some excellent graduate students, including Atipol Bhanich Supapol, Lin Bian, Ron Corvari, Aming He, Ashish Lall, Derek Olmstead, Mohammed Raffiquzzaman, and Eftichios Sartzetakis. He also learned a great deal from discussions at various times with colleagues Stephen Ferris, Soo Bin Park, Tom Ross and, of course, the late John McManus.

Gilles Paquet is an economic historian and a specialist in institutional economics and governance. He has also done extensive work in the media. He taught in the Department of Economics at Carleton from 1963 to 1981. He later joined what is now the Telfer School of Management at the University of Ottawa, where he created the Centre on Governance in 1997. He has been President of the Royal Society of Canada, and he is a Member of the Order of Canada. His website is found at www. gillespaquet.org

Georg Rich taught economics at Carleton from 1967 to 1977, and served as chairman of Carleton's economics department from 1972 to 1974. He joined the Swiss National Bank in 1977 and was appointed as its chief economist in 1985. After his retirement from the SNB in 2001, he became an honorary professor of the University of Bern, and also taught a course at the Graduate Institute of International and Development Studies in Geneva. He has published widely on monetary matters, including studies on the Eurocurrency markets, Canadian monetary history and Swiss monetary policy.

About the Centre on Governance of the University of Ottawa

The Centre on Governance (COG) was created by Gilles Paquet at the end of 1997 as a joint venture of the Faculty of Administration (now the Telfer School of Management) and the Faculty of Social Sciences at the University of Ottawa. From its inception, it was seen as an umbrella organization – a hub for the work on governance taking place in all the faculties of the University of Ottawa. The main objectives of the Centre were to develop: conceptual frameworks for analyzing coordination problems, tools to better analyze governance issues, and a critical approach for repairing governance failures. It was meant to bring together persons who are committed to seeking better responses to contemporary problems of governance in the private, public and civic sectors both within and outside of the University of Ottawa. It aimed from the beginning to be an observatory of emerging trends and experiments in the world of governance.

From the beginning, the COG has been responsible for the publication of *www.optimumonline.ca* – a refereed quarterly on governance and public management. Fellows of the Centre have produced hundreds of papers over the years and generated large numbers of books published under different banners. What follows is a list of the main books and reports produced by the Centre, under the banner of the University of Ottawa Press, then under the banner of Invenire – The Idea Factory, and also under the banners of other publishers. All these books are available from www.amazon.ca.

The University of Ottawa Press (1999-2010)

D. McInnes. 1999. *Taking it to the Hill – The Complete Guide to Appearing before Parliamentary Committees*

G. Paquet. 1999. *Governance through Social Learning*

L. Cardinal & C. Andrew (sld). 2001. *La démocratie à l'épreuve de la gouvernance*

L. Cardinal & D. Headon (eds.). 2002. *Shaping Nations – Constitutionalism and Society in Australia and Canada*

P. Boyer *et al.* (eds.). 2004. *From Subjects to Citizens – A hundred years of citizenship in Australia and Canada*

C. Andrew *et al.* (eds.). 2005. *Accounting for Culture – Thinking though Cultural Citizenship*

G. Paquet. 2005. *The New Geo-Governance: A Baroque Approach*

J. Roy. 2005. *E-government in Canada*

C. Rouillard *et al.* 2006. *Re-engineering the State – Toward an Impoverishment of Quebec Governance*

E. Brunet-Jailly (ed.). 2007. *Borderlands – Comparing Border Security in North America and Europe*

R, Hubbard & G. Paquet. 2007. *Gomery's Blinders and Canadian Federalism*

N. Brown & L. Cardinal (eds.). 2007. *Managing Diversity – Practices of Citizenship*

J. Roy. 2007. *Business and Government in Canada*

T. Brzustowski. 2008. *The Way Ahead – Meeting Canada's Productivity Challenge*

G. Paquet. 2008. *Tableau d'avancement – Petite ethnographie interprétative d'un certain Canada français*

P. Schafer. 2008. *Revolution or Renaissance – Making the transition from an economic age to a cultural age*

G. Paquet. 2008. *Deep Cultural Diversity – A Governance Challenge*

L. Juillet & K. Rasmussen. 2008. *A la défense d'un idéal contesté – le principe de mérite et la CFP 1908-2008*

L. Juillet & K. Rasmussen. 2008. *Defending a Contested Ideal – Merit and the Public Service Commission 1908-2008*

C. Andrew *et al.* (eds.). *Gilles Paquet – Homo Hereticus*

O.P. Dvivedi *et al.* (eds.). 2009. *The Evolving Physiology of Government – Canadian Public Administration in Transition*

G. Paquet. 2009. *Crippling Epistemologies and Governance Failures – A Plea for Experimentalism*

M. Small. 2009. *The Forgotten Peace – Mediation at Niagara Falls 1914*

R. Hubbard & G. Paquet. 2010. *The Black Hole of Public Administration*

P. Dutil *et al.* 2010. *The Service State: Rhetoric, Reality, and Promises*

G. DiGiacomo & M. Flumian (eds.). 2010. *The Case for Centralized Federalism*

R. Hubbard & G. Paquet (eds.). 2010. *The Case for Decentralized Federalism*

Invenire (2009-2017)

R. Higham. 2009. *Who do we think we are: Canada's reasonable (and less reasonable) accommodation debates*

R. Hubbard. 2009. *Profession: Public Servant*

G. Paquet. 2009. *Scheming Virtuously: The Road to Collaborative Governance*

J. Bowen (ed.). 2009. *The Entrepreneurial Effect: Ottawa*

F. Lapointe. 2011. *Cities as Crucibles: Reflections on Canada's Urban Future*

J. Bowen. 2011. *The Entrepreneurial Effect: Waterloo*

G. Paquet. 2011. *Tableau d'avancement II – Essais exploratoires sur la gouvernance d'un certain Canada français*

R. Chattopadhyay & G. Paquet (eds.). 2011. *The Unimagined Canadian Capital – Challenges for the Federal Capital Region*

P. Camu. 2011. *La Flotte Blanche – Histoire de la Compagnie de la navigation du Richelieu et d'Ontario 1845-1913*

M. Behiels & F. Rocher (eds.). 2011. *The State in Transition – Challenges for Canadian Federalism*

R. Clément & C. Andrew (eds.). 2012. *Cities and Languages: Governance and Policy – International Symposium*

R. Clément & C. Andrew (sld). 2012. *Villes et langues : gouvernance et politiques – Symposium international*

C.M. Rocan. 2012. *Challenges in Public Health Governance: The Canadian Experience*

T. Brzustowski. 2012. *Why we need more innovation in Canada and what we must do to get it*

C. Andrew *et al.* 2012. *Gouvernance comunautaire : innovations dans le Canada français hors Québec*

M. Gervais. 2012. *Challenges of Minority Governments in Canada*

R. Hubbard *et al.* (eds.). 2012. *Stewardship: Collaborative decentred metagovernance and inquiring systems*

G. Paquet. 2012. *Moderato cantabile: Toward principled governance for Canada's immigration policy*

G. Paquet & T. Ragan. 2012. *Through the Detox Prism: Exploring organizational failures and design responses*

G. Paquet. 2013. *Tackling Wicked Policy Problems: Equality, Diversity, and Sustainability*

G. Paquet. 2013. *Gouvernance corporative : une entrée en matières*

G. Paquet. 2014. *Tableau d'avancement III – Pour une diaspora canadienne-française antifragile*

R. Clément & P. Foucher. 2014. *50 years of official bilingualism: challenges, analyses and testimonies*

R. Clément & P. Foucher. 2014. *50 ans de bilinguisme official : défis, analyses et témoignages*

R. Hubbard & G. Paquet. 2014. *Probing the Bureaucratic Mind: About Canadian Federal Executives*

G. Paquet. 2014. *Unusual Suspects: Essays on Social Learning Disabilities*

R. Hubbard & G. Paquet. 2015. *Irregular Governance: A Plea for Bold Organizational Experimentation*

L. Cardinal & P. Devette (eds.). 2015. *Autour de Chantal Mouffe – Le politique en conflit*

R. Higham. 2015. *What would you say? … as guest speaker at the next Canadian citizenship ceremony*

D. Gordon. 2015. *Town and Crown – An Illustrated History of Canada's Capital*

G. Paquet & R.A. Perrault. 2016. *The Tainted-Blood Tragedy in Canada: A Cascade of Governance Failures*

G. Paquet & C. Wilson. 2016. *Intelligent Governance: A Prototype for Social Coordination*

R. Hubbard & G. Paquet. 2016. *Driving the Fake Out of Public Administration: Detoxing HR in the Canadian Federal Public Sector*

Christopher Maule (ed.). 2017. *A Future for Economics: More Encompassing, More Institutional, More Practical*

Editions Liber

G. Paquet. 1999. *Oublier la Révolution tranquille – Pour une nouvelle socialité*

G. Paquet. 2004. *Pathologies de gouvernance – Essais de technologie sociale*

G. Paquet. 2005. *Gouvernance : une invitation à la subversion*

G. Paquet. 2008. *Gouvernance : mode d'emploi*

G. Paquet. 2011. *Gouvernance collaborative : un anti-manuel*

Éditions Vrin

P. Laurent & G. Paquet. 1998. *Épistémologie et économie de la relation – coordination et gouvernance distribuée*

Éditions H.M.H.

G. Paquet & J.P. Wallot. 2007. *Un Québec moderne 1760-1840 : Essai d'histoire économique et sociale*

Government of Canada

G. Paquet. 2006 (en collaboration). *The National Capital Commission: Charting a New Course*

Report of the NCC Mandate Review Panel

Special research reports

J. Roy and C. Wilson. 1998. *Strategic Localism and Competitive Advantage*

COG. 1999. *Corporate Governance & Spin-in Ventures*

COG. 1999. *The Borough Model: Municipal Restructuring for Ottawa*

COG. 2000. *The Governance of the Ethical Process for Research – A study for the Tri-council*

COG. 2000. *Governance in the 21st Century*, Lead role in the annual symposium of the RSC

G. Paquet. 2001. *Si Montfort m'était conté ... Essais de pathologie administrative et de rétroprospective*

Talentworks Project (under the supervision of Christopher Wilson)

COG. 2001. *Evaluating TalentWorks: Creating a Foundation for Successful Collaboration*

COG. 2002. *Ottawa's Workforce Environment, Report I of Ottawa Works: A Mosaic of Ottawa's Economic and Workforce Landscape*

COG. 2002. *Profiling Ottawa's Workforce, Report II of Ottawa Works: A Mosaic of Ottawa's Economic and Workforce Landscape*

COG. 2002. *Ottawa's Workforce Development Strategy, Report III of Ottawa Works: A Mosaic of Ottawa's Economic and Workforce Landscape*

A. Chaiton and G. Paquet (eds.). 2002. *Ottawa 2020 – A synthesis of the Smart Growth Summit*

G. Paquet and Kevin Wilkins. 2002. *Ocean governance ... An inquiry into stakeholding*

B. Collins, *et al.* 2003. *Assessment of Public Internet Access in Ottawa: Report of Key Findings*

COG. 2003. *SmartCapital Evaluation Guidelines Report*

COG. 2003. *SmartCapital Baseline Assessment*

R. Hubbard, G. Paquet and C. Wilson. 2004. *CIPO: Reaching the World of SMEs*

COG. 2004. *SmartCapital: A Smart Community Assessment*

G. Paquet and J. Roy. 2005. *CIPO as an Innovation Catalyst*

www.ingramcontent.com/pod-product-compliance
Lightning Source LLC
Chambersburg PA
CBHW062103270326
41931CB00013B/3191